My Journey on
the Mississippi Road

My Journey on the Mississippi Road

How I Survived in the Old Mississippi

J.L. McCullough

VANTAGE PRESS
New York

My Journey on
the Mississippi Road

One

I was born into a family of seven children, five boys and two girls. My sister, Eeula B., was the oldest; I was the second, my brother Willot was third, W.E.L. was fourth, Clarence was fifth, Sally was sixth, and Tommie Lee was seventh. I was born on what is now called the Simpson Road. At that time it was just a plain dirt road. I can recall some of the incidents that happened during that time because I lived there until I was between four and five years old. One of the incidents that's outstanding was when my half brother, Levoy, came to change clothes there and I was playing in the doors. He went in and closed the door on my fingers. I yelled and he opened the door. I ran across the hall into the dining room and I ran straight into the table over there and started my nose to bleeding. My nose has been bleeding ever since; occasionally it does now.

Another thing that I recall was the water we had there wasn't good to wash white clothes in. So, my mother used to go down to Mr. Albert Moore's to wash clothes. I would always go with her. Mr. Moore had what was known as a dug well. It had to have been about four and a half, five feet in diameter. I recall climbing up to try to look into the well. Mother yelled at me and that scared me down. And of course, now looking back I can see why it was dangerous for a young child like that to climb up and try to look into the well like that.

Now, controversies in my life began with me when I was first born. My grandmother wanted to name me Jessie Lee Britain after a great fighter in the community. My mother didn't like that. So, my father wanted to name me after Bishop Moreland and he said he would buy him some more land. And he did! And my mother didn't like that. So, what she did, she sent two letters "J.L." That's the name she sent into the state department. Of course, we lived there until we went to Mobile. My father was a Methodist preacher. But before we went to Mobile, he was a farmer there. He would do all of his hauling and plowing with horses and mules; that was the power that they used at the time. He would park his wagon out near a tree and take the bed off and turn it upside down. For some reason the in gate would always be out. And then he would push the wagon off in the pond and that would keep the wheels tight on the wagon. If you let the wagon set out in the sun the wheels would get loose, when you got ready to haul they would be coming apart. That was protection for the wagon. We would play underneath the wagon bed.

About this time we were about to depart for Mobile. My father had bought a '26 "T" Model Ford. He drove our family to Mobile in that car. We didn't stay down there a long time. We were down there for a short while. I think we enrolled in school there. I had a chance to see a movie down there. It was Cowboys and Indians. It was a good picture! That was the first time I had seen a picture and it was a long time before I saw another one. I think I was going on fifteen when I saw the next movie. But anyway while we were there, I ran into some more boys there and you know how you do in different communities. The word had gotten around to my mother that it was one bad little boy there, and his name was Jimmy Lee. Jimmy Lee was just doing little mischievous things and Mother didn't like for us to play with him. But somehow or another we found time to play with him anyway. And it was another boy named Robert. He was a large boy. You know how kids are around big boys. And for some reason Robert died. It was said he died from eating poisoned plums or maybe they was green. I don't remember what was the cause of death, but I do know that he died and we were all sorry about losing Robert because we all liked him. He was a big boy and we all wanted to be affiliated with him.

As time went on, I remember buying candy. The candy would have a ring in it. It only cost a penny and so we would go to my mother and get some money to go to the store. She would always tell us to be careful. We had all been to the store before. But this time we went, we came to a street that was a busy street at that time. I was walking ahead of my brother and sister and I saw a car coming. It was a way up the street. I decided to go on across. So, I ran on across. I thought my sister and brother were going to follow, but they didn't. They stayed behind and when they didn't come, I decided to run back over there where they were. And I did. . . . Started anyway. But before I could get across the street, the car caught me and it hit me. Even though the driver had slowed down to a speed where it didn't do a thing but bruise me a little, it tore my new brown and blue sweater. I was really upset about the car tearing my new sweater. But I wasn't upset by him running into me! So, finally we got over that.

Not too long after that, we were headed to Mississippi. We came through Demopolis, Alabama. We crossed a river on a ferryboat. That was the first and last time I crossed a river on a ferryboat. While we were in Mobile, my father had bought some land and had a new house built on it. It was a five-room house. When we moved back to Mississippi, my brother, Willot and I had a chance to visit our grandmother, Hattie. She told us how she saved her master's life on the plantation when she was a slave. When the Union soldiers would come to a plantation, they would demand the money from the owner. And if the owner didn't give them the money, they would hang him. The Union soldiers had my grandmother's master outside with the rope around his neck demanding his money. She ran out there and said to them, "Don't kill Master, please! Master don't have no money! Mr. George took all of Master money and went to Texas with it!" And they released him.

While we were at my grandmother's house she would always give us some of the grapes that she grew in her garden. We wanted to visit her every year especially during the grape season. Then Grandmother started visiting us once or twice a year. When she would visit us in the fall, she always wanted one of us to sleep with her. There was always a fight between my brother, Willot and I about who was going to sleep with her. We fought over who would wait on our grandmother . . . who would unlace her shoes or bring her a glass of water. So, I was the one that had a chance to sleep with her. You have no idea how much it meant to me to sleep with my grandmother.

Now, this was a new community that we moved into. We enrolled in school there. It was a one-room school as well as a church. At that time we had school and church in one building. And of course, we were in class with some of the large children. You had to be in class with some of the large children since we were all in a one-room school. For my part, I was *just trying* to learn how to write. Some of those older boys, one was named James Vaughan, but we called him 'Bird Jack' and Isadore Baker, they were able to do their work. I was trying to keep up with them and at the same time, I was learning *how* to write. That *really* put a strain on me. I would go in the spelling class sometimes so nervous I could hardly hold a pencil in my hand. Another thing that hindered me too, my mother had changed my handwriting. That made a difference. I always say that any time a child picks up a pencil and starts writing you should never change his way of holding a pencil. Therefore, all of these things came upon me.

Now the school board had decided that they were going to change teachers. Mr. Rimmer and his granddaughter, Adeline Broomfield, were working at the time. Ms. Broomfield would always open up the devotion with "Old Rugged Cross." She could really sing that! Really she was a beautiful lady and all the little boys on campus were sweet on her. I even said when I got to be a man I was going to marry her! I wouldn't express that to the other boys because I didn't want them to feel the same way. After the board got rid of Mr. Rimmer, Ms. Adeline left, too. So, I was really sad and really hurt over that. I guess it was a long time before I got over it. I didn't see Ms. Adeline anymore. I was seventy years old when I saw her again. She moved over in Holmes County. That's where, I suppose, she stayed all of her life.

But then Mrs. Ophelia Barnes came. Now, during all this time the boys would always have a game to play. Shooting marbles was the big thing then! Every boy you saw had a sack of marbles somewhere on him. One of the famous things was to hang them on the button on your overalls in a tobacco sack. And that's the way we would carry our marbles around. And of course, when we were shooting marbles there were a couple of boys on the campus that would fight everyday! That was Clenoyd Barnes and Louis Fleming. Sometimes a boy called Moreless would fight. I mean they would fight everyday! And another boy, his name was Heywood Taylor; we called him Pont. He would fight with Louis. Out of those four boys one of them was fighting with Louis. So when one of them would get the best of Louis, he would get up and tell him, "I'm going home and get my shotgun and I'll come back. I'm gone blow you dim brains out!" That's the way he said it! Of course, we always said he was trying to say 'damn,' but he couldn't say it. He was so mad or upset that he couldn't say it. So, we joked him about it. I joked him but he never did bother me. I guess he liked me. But one reason he did like me, I was a good marble shooter. I could really shoot marbles! Everybody wants to beat the best shooter. Most of the time I was the best shooter. And I could call myself the champ. Everybody wants to play the champ.

Now, during this time another game came about. It was called, "Mama Peg." It was played with a two-blade knife. You were supposed to throw the knife with the two blades open. Now some of the boys had knives on the campus then, but all of them didn't have knives. Maybe one or two would have them. We would get there with the knife and play that game. There was a point system, so this is how we kept score. If the shorter blade stuck into the ground, you got 100 points. If the longer blade stuck in the ground, you got 50 points. If both blades stuck in the ground you got 75 points. The object of the game was to get to 500 points. If you got to 500 first you were declared the winner. If it was only two players in the game then the one to get to 500 first would have to drive the peg into the ground or if we were in a building we would drive it into a crack in the floor. If it was two or more, then the game would be played until only one player was left. The one that was left would have to route the peg. And if he couldn't route the peg, he couldn't play. What we would do was to drive a piece of wood, the peg, which was two and a half inches long, in the ground, and if the loser could route it up or get it out with his teeth, then he could not play. So that was the type of things that was going on at that time. Now later on the community decided they wanted to have a school. They wanted to build a school. And they did! They got together and they built a school. They used rough lumber; there wasn't any smooth lumber like it is now. They didn't have the money to buy it anyway. But anyway, when they built the school, there were cracks in the floor. If it rained we would circle round in the back corner from where the teacher was. And we played "Mama Peg" right there in the building. And they didn't know what we were doing because you know how boys keep up a lot of noise anyway. We would have a lot of fun. And so, on one particular day, my best friend, Johnny Edwards, he lost to me. He thought he was so smart! He set the peg up in one of the really tight spots in one of the cracks. Fortunately for me, I tapped that peg until it was in so tight that he couldn't pull it out. And of course, we wouldn't let him play. And that was really the biggest laugh we had that day!

During this time, Mrs. Ophelia Barnes was teaching and it must have been some kind of government program. I think it was her sister; her name was Lovie Carson. She used to come and bring cocoa to the school for lunch. When it rained a lot of children wouldn't come to school. But we had raincoats and could always go. So when we would get to school on a rainy day our chances of getting two or two and a half cups of cocoa were really good. And we would not miss a day when it rained for anything because we enjoyed that cocoa so much! One day on my way to school I was ambushed! The Clerk boys had it in for me.

I was walking to school on this particular morning and I saw Eddie Clerk and his cousin, Noah coming up the road.

I said, "Hey, fellows, what's up?"

I noticed then that Eddie had an axe in his hand and his cousin came up to me. He said, "You better not raise your hands or I'm gone knock your brains out." He held the axe up high and Noah proceeded to whip me all the way to school! Well, when we got to school, I was mad. But there wasn't nothing I could do about it with them holding an axe on me. Now, I knew that Noah was going to ask to be excused.

See, we didn't have indoor plumbing in the school. However, what we did have was a deep ditch about forty feet deep that we used for an outhouse. What we did, we climbed down into it and did our business and then we had to climb out. Well, I knew that ole Noah would ask to go to the ditch. So, I told my friend, Johnny Edwards to back me up. When Noah asked to go to the ditch, then I was gone ask after he went. If his cousin asked to go after I went, then Johnny was supposed to ask to go. Now that's exactly what happened. Noah went to the ditch and his cousin, Eddie, knew I was going to get him back for the whipping I had taken that morning all the way to school. So, when I asked to go, Eddie asked after I had left the room. Johnny came out after him. When I got out there, I figured Noah should be coming up out of the ditch about that time and when he stepped up out of the ditch I met him with my fist. BAM! I hit him right smack in the face and down he went back into the ditch. Sure enough, Johnny held off Noah Clerk's cousin so that they wouldn't double-team me.

During that time agents would travel through the community to churches and schools and let them sell candy for different projects. Each church had a different project. Our project was the basketball. We sold candy and he came back and bought the basketball and John Henry Clerk was the boy's name, and he taught us how to make goals out of hoops of small barrels. And that introduced us to basketball. You know, we played out on the ground. I don't know if anybody had a gymnasium at that time. That's how he introduced us to basketball. Of course, we were all happy about that. Things started to happen around there. I started playing baseball. Well, baseball had gotten really popular because that was during the era of Babe Ruth and everybody wanted to be like Babe Ruth; they wanted to hit a homerun. But we didn't have the money to buy the equipment with. So, what we had to do was make everything we used. We didn't have gloves. The boy behind the plate, the catcher, would usually take his jumper off (the jumper was made out of the same thing as his overalls) and make a good mitt. Then to make the ball we would use some fishing cord. Sometimes we played with a rubber ball. We would take the fishing cord and wind it up to make the size ball we wanted. Then we would put a cover on it. We got the cover from a shoe. Most of the time we would cut the tongue out of the shoes we were wearing and use that to cover the ball! Of course, whoever furnished the ball was the boss of the game. He would tell you who could play and tell you where you could play and give us the batting order and everything. He was just like a manager and an owner of a regular baseball team. So that's what we started doing then. Of course, we all liked that because we were getting larger at that time.

And of course, about that time, my father was calling on us to start working in the fields. We were large enough. So, what we did was, we would go home in the evening and on Saturday, he would tell us to knock the stalk. That would be early in February, so then across the winter the stalk would be brittle and you could hit it with a stick. That's what we did, break them off and make it easy for the turning plow to cover them up. That was our job.

Two

Of course, during that time we were having programs. I had good friends there: C.M. Boulden, Clenoyd Barnes, and Author Mabry. We had all decided that we wanted to learn how to 'hobo.' At that time people were always talking about hobos coming through the community all the time. So, there were three cars in the community at that time. And those three cars belonged to Thaddeus Rimmer, Marshall Body, and Buddy Madison. They would come to the school to the programs at night and then we would catch on to the spare tire and put our foot on the bumper. Back at that time, you could catch on and ride easily because you held onto the spare tire. And that's what we did. The one that would ride the farthest would be the best rider. That's the kind of thing we did for fun for a little while until something happened later on and we stopped riding.

Now it was something that I mentioned to you earlier. My parents had trouble choosing my name. And I never found out until my half sister, Trudy, came to stay with us. She and her husband had had a fight and she came home and she was there and she brought her three children. Her oldest girl was Earlee, next one was Willameta, and the boy was called D.C. While she was there we were out working somewhere on some kind of project, she brought it up to me. She told me about my name. She said, "Your name is not Moreland. Your name is J.L." And I said, "No." And she explained to me what happened. Of course, when she explained it to me, I was just as happy as I could be to have the same initials as a distant cousin with the initials J.L. His name was J.L. Jones and mine was J.L. McCullough. From then on I proceeded to use that name, J.L.

About this time, my father had started me to work more in the field. Of course, when it was time for him get his crop in he started me to harrowing. That's the first thing I can remember doing. And during that time a particular plow was used called the Oliver Turning Plow. A new point was introduced and it was called a scraper point. That scraper would cut the row down so narrow that whoever was hoeing didn't have as much of a row to cover. That made it much easier on the people who were hoeing. We really enjoyed that! Back then in the fall when the farmers got through gathering the crops they would turn out the cows and each family would put a bell on their cows and that way they would always know where to find them. So we had to get the cows up and milk them. I was old enough, also, to make a fire. I started making fires in the fireplace and Mother wanted me to make a fire in the stove. And my brother would make a fire in the fireplace. So, across the summer we would cut wood to take to the kitchen for cooking. Then we would cut wood for the fireplace for heat.

That summer we would also cut wood to make up syrup with. My daddy had a molasses mill and he cooked syrup for everyone in the community. He taught me to cook syrup, too. The first thing you have to learn is how to skim the syrup when it begins cooking. If you keep the skim off of it well, your molasses would be just as clear as honey. And that's what we had to do. He also taught me how to runoff the syrup when it was done. Now we would always bring the cane to the mill because we had to grind the cane. He taught me the whole works. After that, we would have to get the cows up and milk them. We could go get them in the evenings sometimes. We had an old cow there and she was a good milk cow. She was mixed with Holstein and Jersey; she had to be. That old cow was named Mary; I never will forget her. She would have rich milk and she was a good butter cow. My mother always wanted us to milk that cow. But that cow was so mean that we just hated to milk her. If we could possibly do it we would omit bringing her up. Then way over in the night she would come to the house. We would have to go milk her anyway. We hated it so bad! She got so bad until we had to start tying her head. We tied her to two trees. It seemed like these trees were planted for her. We tied one chain around her neck and tied it to one tree and put the other one on her hind legs and tied it to the other tree. That's the way we had to milk her. And during the times the weather was cold, we had so much trouble. We hated it so much but we always had to milk that cow. I was so glad when we got rid of her I didn't know what to do!

On the farm, your horses were kept in the stables and you had to clean them out. The waste taken from the stable is what we would take to the garden and to the watermelon patch. That's what we would use as fertilizer. Then if he had more than he needed for that, then he would find a poor spot in the field and fertilize there. That's how we got fertilizer. Now my father was real good when it came to doing things like that.

We also raised corn. Mr. Shelby Dendy had a mill. And we always would shell the corn to take to the mill on Saturdays. One of Mr. Dendy's wedge hands ran the mill. His name was Captain. We called him that; I don't know what his real name was. Captain Clerk ran the mill. We would shell the corn and we would get to the mill by eight o'clock. So many people would come to the mill; sometimes it would be two and three o'clock before we left for home. The boys would be up there shooting marbles and of course, when your turn came Captain Clerk would come out and call us in. Then we would go in to get our corn ground and take it home. During that time, there was a white gentleman up there called Sam Buewell. His boys would come to the mill. They would always drive oxen. We decided we all wanted oxen. We finally got a pair. We got an ox yoke and trained us some oxen, too. About the time we got them trained, my daddy decided he would kill one of them for beef. Therefore, he left us without oxen to pull our wagon. My dad had a young bull. He was wild, and he wasn't big enough to kill so we had to take him and try to train him. We were never able to train that bull. We just *couldn't* train him. We worked and worked with him until we got tired and gave up on him. We let him go.

During this time, a lady and her son and her son's wife and two children moved near us. They came to be close to my mother. She would always cook something for Mother and Mother would cook something for her. Her son was a hunter. He would go squirrel hunting and coon hunting and different things like that. It so happened early one summer after they had used up most of the corn in the crib. They were eating rats and we didn't know it. Well, my mother knew her son was a squirrel hunter and thought they were having squirrel to eat. Mrs. Leora Mabry invited Mother up there to eat squirrel with her. She didn't tell her it was rat. When Mother was finished eating the rats that was supposed to have been squirrel, she was talking about how good the squirrel was. Mrs. Leora said, "No, that wasn't squirrel. That was rat, honey." She said, "Son went out there in the barn (she called him Son, but his name was Isaiah) and he killed these big rats and skinned them. That's what we ate to-day." Mother was so outdone because she always talked about nasty rats and how you couldn't give her a rat for anything in the world.

When she came back and told us about it, our corn was low so we went out there and we killed some rats, too! She said if we would skin them she would cook them! And they were *good*! Now people tell you that they want eat rat but if you get rats out of the corn crib, you can't tell them from a squirrel. Just like feeding a hog or a cow with corn, and you feed a cow out and call them corn fed. That's the same way it would be with a rat. That was something we would joke Mother about until we would make her mad and she would make us stop! We always had fun about that.

Time came for one of my friends to come home with me. His name was Clenoyd Barnes but we called him Big Baby all the time. That night a man came to talk to my dad about something. We were out in the yard, all the boys. When he pulled out, we all got on his car like we usually do when a car came in. We stayed a good piece from the road. The rest of the boys got off at the road but I decided to ride on out on the gravel road to show them I was the best rider. I went out there and the car started picking up speed. When I went to get off, somehow or an-other I either fell off or the car threw me. It didn't break any bones; it just bruised me. However, I wound up with a mouth full of rocks. I was knocked out but I wandered my way back to the house. When I got there I said, "Big Baby, when did you come over here?" He had come with me from school . . . that's just to show you how bad I was out of my head. I came to my senses that night. But the next day or two I was spitting up gravel! That was the last time that I rode a car!

Now what was taking place, we were going to Sunday School and sometimes my daddy would catch Mr. Simp Boyd. He had a buggy and he would let us ride. We were just as happy as ducks in a pond to be able to ride in his buggy! While we were going to Sunday School, somehow or another they got to discussing about a mule. My daddy had a mule and Mr. Simp knew about him and his background. We called that old mule Black. Mr. Simp had a young mule close to three years old and he could not break him at his age. He wanted to trade that young mule to my daddy for Old Black. They finally got together and traded. My daddy was getting the young mule because we could break him and we could have a young mule a long time. After my daddy traded with Mr. Simp, we turned the stock out in the fall. Our mule went back to where he was born, back to Mr. Simp Boyd. My daddy ran across Mr. Boyd somewhere and he told my dad the young mule had come back. So, we had to go get him.

On our way down there we ran into Pont. His name was Heywood Taylor. It was three of us and he wanted to knock my brother and me and little Ollie Chambers who was with us. But he was trying to get a hold of *me*. I knew what he was trying to do and I didn't want to run from him. I didn't want him to know that I was afraid of him! So, I had to toughen up and say I would knock him! So usually when we started to knocking (that was boxing, only difference in it and regular boxing was we didn't have gloves and we didn't hit in the face). But that day, when he told us he was "gone knock all three of us" just to get me, I said, "Now, I'm gone have to do something!" So, this is what I did. When we started boxing, we usually started tapping, just like regular boxers do, punching lightly. But that time I didn't punch lightly! I drew back and I hit him somewhere in his ribs. I cut his wind off and you would think I had a rope around his neck choking him! That was the way I was able to get away from there without any more abuse.

Sometime later on, we were coming from a baptizing over there at Mr. Terrell Fulton's pond. Pont came up. He was going to get even with me for the time I whipped him before down there. I didn't want to be bothered with him. I was afraid he was gone catch me and really whip me! When he caught up with me and started using abusive language, telling me what he was gone do, I looked over there and saw a stick. Look like I saw the stick just as he made his aggressive move to come toward me. I didn't want to hit him on the head. I didn't want to kill him now or anything like that. I didn't want to hurt him. So I hit him on his leg and when I hit him on his leg he had a rising on that leg and I happened to hit that rising and busted it! When I busted that rising, he stopped to try to stop it from bleeding and I left there.

Mr. Fulton's grandson was on his way to church. I ran up there and caught up with him. His name was Fulton Cannon. That kept Pont from bothering me! I got away from him that time.

In this community, we had gotten acquainted with a white family. Mr. Jim Putnam and my daddy got to be good friends. My daddy would borrow a mule and Mr. Putnam would borrow my daddy's mule and things like that. My mother had washing problems with our water and the Putnams had a well with good water. It wasn't deep; it was shallow. I imagine it was about twenty feet deep. It so happened that the women in the community started meeting at the well on the same day. I would draw water for all of them because I enjoyed drawing the water from that well. Now, my brother and I made friends with the Putnams' son. His name was Roy. We used to hunt and fish together.

So, one day we decided we were going to build a boat. They had a nice pond and we were going to build a boat to go out in the pond and fish. We had heard about some of those Parker boys (white boys) meeting Roy out there sometime and beating the black boys up. When we got through with the boat and were pushing it off in the water, somehow or another Roy saw the Parker boys coming. He ran over there to meet them. I saw him when he broke run.

I said, "Roy, what you running for?"

He said, "You had better be running yourself!"

Then I looked up and I saw the boys coming. Well, we didn't think anything about it until the boys came and they started to throw rocks or something at us to try to frighten us. But, that's where they made the mistake. We had the weapons! We had the hammers! We got the hammers and met them. We ran them off and they went back to the Putnams' house and told the older brother. Oh, I reckon he was about fifteen. He came down there and told us to go home and we did. The Putnams' had their mailbox over there near our house. I didn't know about it, but Willot was laying for Roy to come to the mailbox the next day. Roy did come to their mailbox. And when we got over there Willot jumped on Roy and beat him up!

Well, that rocked on for a couple months later while we was on our way from Sunday School and some of the larger white boys met us. I never will forget this ole boy's name, the one that was doing all the talk, they called him Mike. They came up there. I had my younger sisters and brothers with me, my young sister and young brothers, rather. He was talking to us about hitting a white boy . . .

18

didn't we know better? I didn't say nothing; my brother, he talked and said whatever they wanted him to say. Since we couldn't run off and leave our sister we just had to bear along with them until we got to a fork where they turned and went by the Putnams' house and we went home. That was the end of that. My brothers whipped Roy because he had attempted to jump on us with the Parker boys. So I think that was the last time we had any problems. We were always friends from then on.

But the time came during that school year we didn't have any water. We had to go to different wells. We had to go to Mr. John Phillips' house and Mr. Terrell Fulton's to get water. The time came for me to get the water and of course, it was another family that we got to be really close with, the Jones family. His older brother was named Booker T. and my friend was named Harvey. They had a sister named Sally. Harvey and I were about the same age or same size. And we became really good friends and his brother Booker T. taught me how to wrestle because he was one of the best wrestlers. Nobody around there could throw him. That's one reason I liked the Jones family. That gave us an opportunity to get even closer by us becoming the water boys.

Time came for me to go home with Clenoyd Barnes, Big Baby, we called him. They had moved to a community called Evening Star, up in that area. Finally, my mother let me go with him and when I got there that evening, there was some older boys around there talking about, "Well, Pont was gone be up here this evening and he said he was gone get you!" Of course, I did some smart talk because I didn't think Pont was going to be there or that I would be seeing Pont that night. The moon was shining real bright and we kept talking. And finally, we heard somebody talking and knocking on the door. It was Pont! I imagine my eyes got as big as a silver dollar when they said who it was! They pushed it up, the older boys did. But there was nobody to help me then. See, I had bragged and now I had to prove what I could do! I had been telling them how I was gone deal with Pont. So, we got out there and I knew the only chance I had with him since he was the oldest, I had to hit him like I did when we found that mule! So, we got out there and he tapped me lightly. And I drew back again and let him have it all at once. And I hit him so hard, that it choked him. I imagined he stood there two or three minutes before he could breathe and after that I didn't have any more trouble with Pont.

I was so glad to get away from up there the next morning I didn't know what to do! Another incident happened, I must have been near around twelve years old, I guess. I was big for my age and I thought I was a man because I was doing man's work. I wouldn't let the big boys throw me after Booker T. taught me. So, that Sunday came. I went into the house and took a bath and put on my clean clothes. I had on some bellbottoms. Aunt Kate made those pants for me, she wasn't my auntie but her husband was my dad's first wife's brother. So we called them uncle and auntie just like they were my regular auntie and uncle.

I came out that day and I told Mother, I said, "Mother, I'm gone go over to Mrs. Bert Ella's awhile."

She said, "Who said it?" She out done me so bad. She said, "You ain't going nowhere. You better go back in there and pull them clothes off!" And that really got away with me!

My next challenge was my daddy. I told him I was a better farmer than he was. He ought to let me run the farm and he agreed. I had been watching the folks on Mr. Dennis' plantation how they were doing. Now, my dad didn't do it because he didn't buy no fertilizer. I did my work the exact same way they did. During the preparation of the land we got it fixed up and got it planted. And that year I beat my daddy. He would always make about three bales of cotton, really it was four, but what he would do he could put four bales into three and that would save bagging that he had to buy for an extra bale of cotton. He was real close with the dollar. Doing it that way saved him some money from buying an extra bag.

That year, instead of making three bales, I made six. Then my Granddad, my mother's father, Giles Allen, he had some crusty cotton. He gave us enough seed to plant an acre. We planted that on the best land we had. My father saved those seeds and he had enough cotton seed to plant the whole crop the next year. And of course we made real crop again; made six bales again. Therefore, that was my last crop up there. During this time, Herefords came into that community. I don't know where they came from; Mr. Shelby Dennis had a Hereford bull he had bought. Somehow that bull bred one of my dad's cows and the cow had a bull calf. He was a real good looking bull. He had real broad hips and everything, broad-back and we wanted to ride him. So, one day my daddy went to Sunday school and left us there. We decided we were going to ride him. And I did! I went down to the cow pen and my brother helped me catch him. I got on that bull and he got to bucking and carrying on. All of a sudden he started going through the fence! He cut a gash in my thigh about three quarters of an inch deep. Of course, we didn't want my daddy to know about it. All I did was stuck some clay dirt in there; stopped it from bleeding and we went on got that bull and put him back in the pen. The thing that I couldn't keep my dad from knowing, I had tore my pants. That's what I regretted.

After that we were getting ready to move into another community. Daddy had sold his place up there where we were. At that time boys in that community were buying blank pistols. A blank was almost like a twenty-two. It really didn't have any lead in the cartridge but we could take it and stick wire or cut a nail and push it down in there, something to make a cartridge for it. That would be our bullet. We would go out shooting at birds; we didn't have to meddle people or shoot at one another because we always showed the next kid how to make a bullet. We just had fun gently. So when we moved into the new community my grandmother had passed that year. She passed in '36.

My grandfather was at that time living by himself. His name was Jim McCullough and he moved in with us down there. My grandfather told me how he was treated when he was a slave. He also told me about some of the things that he did when he would go out at night. The master had a bad dog. When my grandfather would get to the yard, he would carry a sack with him; he would pull pickets off of the fence and lure the dog into the sack. He would tie the sack and leave the dog out there until he came back. When he came back, he would untie the sack to let the dog back in the yard and replace the pickets on the fence. No one would ever know that he had left the slave quarters. My grandfather also served in the civil war. He had a sword that he used in the war. I don't know what became of that sword.

He took me and showed me how to set out hooks to catch fish. And the first squirrel I saw out in the wilderness he showed it to me. Somehow or another, he felt like he had lived and all of his friends had died and he just didn't want to live. He died that March. Yet, in the meantime when we moved down there, we enrolled in school. It was in December when we moved down there. We had the blank pistols when I went to a new school there. The boys there they came in with paper-caps. I remember Mozell Sanders was the largest boy there before I came. He and his brother, Roosevelt, whom we called Happy, had paper-cap pistols and I had a blank pistol and my brother, Willot, had a blank pistol. So we walked in there, and Mozell saw us and you could see him go down like you punch a hole in a balloon! He just went down when he saw us because I was larger than he was. He *had* been the largest boy in school.

When we got in that community boys didn't go to school much. Most things they did was hunt. Well, when we got there, my daddy had a man that moved down there with us from the delta, Dan Thompson. He was the one who introduced us to what they called a gangplow and we called it a walking cultivator or a one-rope cultivator. After we got out of school each day we would go down there and clean off branches down in the field. He was the head step so, my daddy paid him. We would go down and work and help clean off those ole ditches. In the meantime, the boys around there around the age of twelve or thirteen didn't go to school because this was one of the poorest communities, I believe, emphasizing schools; I suppose it was at that time, in the county. Well, they started to hunting when they get that age.

When I got there, it was a man who lived right there by the school, Paul V. Hardy, and his wife, Mrs. Willie Mae. When we would go to Sunday school, I would go by there and sit and talk with Mrs Willie Mae. She had three daughters at that time, Annie, Willie Bell and Callie. Well, of course, I just would go to Sunday school and if I didn't have anything else to do, I would go by there and sit and talk with Mrs. Willie Mae. So we did that on and on.

So finally, her daughter got large enough for me to start eyeing her. Of course, before long we did start to talking, Annie, the oldest daughter. We rocked around there for a while. So finally we got to being real close. They didn't stay that far from the school, about a hundred yards. I got to liking her and my brother started liking her cousin, Eliza Anderson. My brother and Eliza broke up and Eliza encouraged Annie not to let me walk her home from the party at school that night. That really hurt me cause the boys knew it. You know how boys brag about things. Most of the boys were afraid of Mr. Paul. I wasn't; he was always nice to me. I never did think nothing about him. He had an older son, Josh. He and I were good friends. Josh wasn't going to school. He was about seventeen, I guess, at that time.

This is what happened at the school while I was there. There was a lady who lived across the road from us. She had four children, I believe, and her husband had died. The boys did go to school. And all of a sudden, one in the family had to pick on one. We called this boy Pat. Pat would pick on T.J. every day! He would pick up sweet gum burs off the ground and throw and hit him. So that morning, T.J. stepped up close to me. I didn't move; I just stayed there. Pat threw something over again and he missed T.J. and hit me! And I just stepped over there and I had been telling him to stop every day. So, I just stepped over there and hit him in the face as hard as I could. And his face swelled up and the word passed around the campus that I had hit Pat. All the children started coming toward me. And my father had taught me that if I get to fighting with more than one person don't ever let them come up from behind me; always try to back up to a building. I backed up to the school. Of course, I could hit so hard, they wouldn't charge me. When I hit one of them they would back up. And I did that to keep them off of me until the teacher came out there. When she came out there, I thought everything was settled. Pat's older sister, Willie Mae, she had a chunk in her hand. She threw that chunk and hit me in the back. That was the only lick I got.

So from there, farming time came. I had taken the responsibility and got the crop in with the new cultivator we had there. I was able to manage the crop much more efficiently with that cultivator. We were carrying one row, we could take one row and finish it up and be through with it. So that was a big help there. Mr. Dan Thomas bought one and taught us how to use it. Sometime later another girl moved in the community. Her name was Vanella. I know she stayed with a lady we called Miss Hannah. Vanella was going to school with us at St. Paul. I started talking to her. We were right about the same age. For some reason, we were coming from school when all these boys that weren't going to school would meet us on the road. Vanella and I were arguing about something; I don't know what it was. But anyway, I slapped Vanella and about that time these boys that were up there happened to see it! This ole boy, we called him Hot, he had a shotgun and he didn't have no shells. He was there trying to get a shell. He said he was going to shoot me. I didn't have sense enough to know he could do it. However, he didn't ever get a shell and that broke it up.

So, I started drifting and, of course, my sister was trying to get me to go to school because when she moved down here she was in the tenth grade. Yet, she had decided she was going to get married. When we moved down there she met a boy named James Allen. He and I were good friends. We called him Bo Allen. He and I got along well. In fact, he introduced me to different girls. I think we used to just be around a lot together. This is how some of the love letters sounded that I wrote while I was in the eight grade:

Dearest Dorothy,
In the hills of Mississippi this is a lonesome state. A letter like this don't carry no date. Why sitting between the walls of life and love; It affords me great pleasure to try to inform you a part of my mind. While I sit here thinking about my feelings for you and how can I express it to you, I feel real lonely and hoping that someday that you may come to my exploitations. I will remain with you by my side, forever. This is what I want to say to you, dear, as I watch the sun set in the beautiful evening shadows casting upon you then I wonder how nice it would be to share this time with you . I suppose now that you are tired of reading bad writing. So I will close my letter but not my love. Yours forever, J.L. McCullough.

So, that next December my sister got married. My interest in school went down. My uncle came over here from Durmott, Arkansas, Uncle Charlie. His son, Albert, was in the sixth grade. Well, what he told me was he using some six-grade books and some seventh grade books. That's all I knew. I was in the eight grade and getting up in the age. My uncle said, "Boy, you never gone finish school. You gone start to running with these little girls and that's gone be the end of your school days." Of course, I wanted to make him out a lie and things weren't going well, especially after my sister married. James Allen was not a progressive young man and they didn't stay together long. My sister divorced him and moved downtown Canton with my cousin, C.J. Blount and went to work there. First she started working at a café and then she started working for a fruit store. The man that was running it was named Mr. Ivy. She worked for him for a long time. But anyway, while she was there she was staying with my cousin, C.J. Blount and her husband Howard. She got me interested in coming back to school. That summer while I was out of school we had laid by our crop; she wanted me to come down to Canton. But before I went down there it was a white gentleman named A.R. Parker in Valley View running a store. He had a crop, but he didn't know nothing about farming. He was behind in his crop and he wanted somebody to help him out. So he asked me about it and I talked with a boy we called Jack Mag. Jack did agree to it. So, we went there and we laid his crop by. He paid us $0.25 a day to work.

That's when I really went on downtown with my sister. I ran into a man down there by the name of Hand Montgomery. He wanted somebody to work on his farm. He had a tractor. I went out and drove tractors for him until he got finished. Then I began to work for Alfred Mucker. He was cotton buyer. He taught me how to grade the cotton. My job was to take the cotton to the depot and clean up the building.

My sister was still worrying me about going back to school. So, I decided to go back. I hated to go because I was behind. Then when I *did* decide I said, "Well, I'll just try to enroll in the ninth grade. I've been in the eighth grade long enough." When I got there to go in the ninth grade, all the country children were going to the same school because there was only one school for blacks in Canton. That was Cameron Street High School for blacks. That place was full! That ninth grade class was full and I couldn't enroll in that class. And they put me back in the eighth grade another year. That really hurt me really bad to have to go back to the eighth grade again. To make my uncle out a lie, I didn't have much choice. Everybody talked about an education but it hadn't been of much interest to me. You know I didn't know I would ever need an education and I didn't feel like then that I had to have one.

So I decided to try to put up with being called "Old Man" and everything while I was in school. Of course at that time if you go down to that school, being over-aged, Professor Rodgers didn't worry about it as long as you had good conduct in school. At that time when a boy go to school at that age, he was there to go to school; he wasn't there to be carrying on foolishness like these youngsters do now. He was there to try to get an education. That's what I was there for. Really, whoever did come there was made a better person. They really believed in character building. The way they handled the school there, you had to have real good character if you wanted to be in the luxury clubs. And all the boys that came there, all the older boys like me had to have good character because it would be nothing for them to tell you to go home because you were overaged and down there cutting up. So we were really their model students. I can see now why he would want older boys to come there. We weren't organized in sports like we are now where you can come and play at a certain age for so long. You were there to get an education. When I got in school that year I finished the eighth grade; I went to Navico and started to work down there. I didn't like it but I had made a little money.

I left Navico and went to Memphis and worked at the Memphis Furniture Company. They were a furniture manufacturer. So I bought a few clothes and I came on back and went to school that fall. So, that's what I did and my sister still took care of me. She kept pushing me to go to school. So I did. In school that year, what happened was this. When I was in the eighth grade, I didn't realize how prejudiced the city boys were toward the country boys. I would go out there and they would be playing softball. The ball would come out there and I would get it. I would put my hand on the ball and they would scold me like I'd stolen the governor's white mule. They did that until one day they didn't have enough players and the coach invited me to play. I had a chance to get to bat and there was a man on second and third. I hit a home run. So after that, they stopped scolding me as bad. But, it kept on. The city boys were all well-dressed, and of course most of the country boys dressed common. And I reckon that was one reason why they were so prejudiced against us. During that time, when I was at school and I was in the eighth grade trying to establish myself, we had a mathematical problem involving a cow. The cow was tied to a stake and the question was how far from the stake could she graze. It was simply a circle. I worked on it that weekend until I finally got it. That Monday morning when I came back to school the teacher asked us if any of us worked the problem. I raised my hand. She told me to put it on the board. My teacher's name was Desiree Hoarse. So, I did. During that time, the teacher was coming out of college, but they were not majoring in math and science like they do now. So, the teacher did not know much more about that subject. So that is one of the reasons why I had the opportunity to try to work that problem out without the assistance of a teacher. More or less the teacher was our guide. That gave me a star in my crown there . . . being a scholar.

After school, the boys would be playing basketball. If I would put my hand on the basketball, I was going to get a good scolding. So, one day they didn't have enough men to play a basketball game. The coach was Willie Roy Patton. He was a young man at that time. He had played at Alcorn College in Lorman, Mississippi. He called me and asked me if I wanted to play. I told him I didn't know how. He said, "Well, do you want to play?"

I said, "Yes."

He said, "I'll show you what to do." And he did. They were playing man to man. He said, "McCullough, I want you to guard this man here and don't let him get his hand on the ball." And he proceeded to show me how to do it.

I did it! That man didn't get his hand on the ball anymore! So after the game was over he said, "I thought you could not play?"

I said, "Well I have never played before in my life so there was no reason to think I could play." He said that I did well. Eventually, I made the team. Some of those boys that had been there left and went to the army. I finally played a game once up in Louise, up in the Delta. We went up there and won that game. I don't remember us going to another school. It wasn't organized like it is now.

Three

So when school was out that year, somehow or another I got in touch with Josh Hardy. He was working in Gulf Port where they were building that air base. He carried me down there and got a room for me where he was rooming. He got a job for me at the airbase. I went to work at the airbase. I didn't know anything but work. We were the labor hands and they didn't allow us to be nothing but laborers at that time. I was always the fellow that liked to be doing something. So, when the foreman would come and ask for somebody to go clean out a building that's all we were doing; handling material and cleaning outbuildings, things like that. So, I'd always volunteer and it got to the place where they said they don't want me, they wanted somebody else. I didn't know what they were building up. He told me I want you to go and get a bucket and get some water for these men. He had some boys getting water and they were too sorry to get the ice and put in it. They had ice in a barrel and he said I could go out there and fill up my buckets with ice and keep the water cold and those boys were to sorry to do that. I went over there and I got that bucket and I filled it up with ice with just a little water so cold you couldn't drink it.

I worked like that for a while. The carpenters wanted me to work for them. The foreman for the carpenter group had to be pretty tight with the superintendent in order to get things done like he wanted. I worked with a bunch of carpenters for a while. Then the finish carpenters decided they wanted me to work for them. Well it wasn't but three of them. I would go out there and fill that bucket with ice and put a little water on it. It stayed cold all day. So, we got to talking around there and of course they were telling me things that happened. We just got to be really good friends. I got up there and they were finishing putting in windows. I knew I could do that. I had been working in the shop a little. I grew up on a farm and doing one thing or another.

So, I would stand around there watching them. I could do anything they could do. Well, he let me fix some windows while he smoked a cigarette. I got started and he said, "Don't let the boss catch you, now." They had me over there, I didn't have nothing to do. I got up there and did whatever he was doing and did it better than he could. "Just don't let the boss catch you." And I didn't. And he said, "We'll be watching too."

So, if they were working and I didn't have anything to do, I would go over there and go to sleep. They said, "We will wake you up if we see the boss coming." And they did. So, I ran into a gentleman from Leake County. He had a crop there and he started talking to me when he found out I was from Madison County. He wanted me to go back and help him to gather his crop. Well, I didn't tell him I wouldn't, I knew I wasn't. I was going back to school. So, I let him make up all the dates and he told me when we would leave. About a week before that time, I left and went back to go to school. So, I was a little better dressed that year.

So, it rocked on and I went back to school and I was dressed pretty good. I was looked upon a little better even if I wasn't quite accepted there. While I was down in Gulf Port I ran upon one of those carpenters and he told me about the military and that he was a guns mate. I wanted to get in the Navy. He told me about it. He said, "One thing about the Navy, you won't ever be hungry because they have food on that ship at all times." He really impressed me so about being a guns mate that I figured at that time I could get one of those big guns and whip the Japanese by myself. So I was really hot to be a guns mate.

When I got back to school that year, I was in the ninth grade. Looked like they were going call me. My carpenter friend had told me to volunteer. When the Army got ready to call me, then I was supposed to volunteer. So, that is what I did. My number was getting close. Me and another boy, Cleveland Parker, lived in the city. We decided we would volunteer. Well, we went down there, however, he didn't pass the military test; I did. I was thinking I was going to have some time to come back like the guys in the Army did. At that time, when you were drafted, you were given thirty days before you went in. But I didn't know that if you volunteered you didn't get any time.

So, I prepared myself that I was going to come back home. They told me that I couldn't go back home. I was told I was going to Great Lakes, Illinois. That's where I was *supposed* to go. Of course, they had gotten a little bit liberal at the time that I was going up there. I was trying so hard to get in because this fellow had influenced me so about the Navy. However, I ran into a problem. We were getting ready to catch the train but Cleveland didn't pass so he went on back home. I had to leave that night for the Navy. Some boys there had two or three years in college. They were also going into the Navy. One old boy there, I knew he had only a fourth- or fifth-grade-level education. He was loud and boisterous. That's who they picked to put over us. And at that time, white people didn't encourage black boys to become educated. They always tried to show us where our education was no good. Therefore, they didn't pick one of the boys that was better prepared to lead the group.

When we got to the train, I got ready to get on. That's when it all started. All of the other boys that walked up there they would hand them their papers. I handed him mine. He said, "You step aside."

I wondered what was wrong. So after all those boys got on I told the officer, "Well, I was supposed to go to Great Lakes."

He said, "These papers aren't any good here. I'm going to make you out some more." And he did. He made me out some more papers and he said, "You are going to North Folk, Virginia." You could have seen the change on me. I felt so sick I just didn't know what to do. I was sick enough to die.

I went on up there and of course, they put us in there and started to try to train us. I was always able to do things. But the first thing in the morning when you get up, they would come over there and call for volunteers to clean the head. That was the restroom. I would always volunteer. I did that so often until when they would come they would say, "We don't want you. We want somebody else." At that time they gave me papers that let me go on leave anytime I wanted. I was so sick of being there because I didn't have no intention of being no mess attendant. I didn't want to be in no kitchen; I didn't want to serve nobody. I wanted to just be a gun's mate. Therefore, I was sick. So, eventually, by me being sick all the time, they sent me to a hospital. They sent a bunch of the boys to the hospital. They had what they called short arm inspection. A lot of boys were found to have gonorrhea. They cured them all. I stayed on there in that hospital until

34

they decided they were going to give me a medical discharge.

I came on back home in March of that year and started back to school. While in school, I ran into a boy that was going to school there. His name was John Dancy Woodard. He was way up in his grade. He must have been in the eleventh grade. He and I became good friends. Now, his folks had a car. In many cases, we would use it.

I reckon the school gave me credit for the time I lost while I was in the Navy. I came back and my sister had a house then and I finished the year living with her. After that, I met a fellow by the name of Joseph Powell. He was from Meadville, Pennsylvania. I went with him up there and he got a room for me up there. The rooming house was noisy; we had a jukebox. It was sure enough noisy on the weekend. I got tired of that. While I was there I met a fellow named Ramon. We were working on the highway. He was telling me about New Jersey. I was getting ninety cent an hour in Pennsylvania working on the highway.

But, before I left Canton, I was working in the Mansion Mill at night until school was out. That's how I got the money to travel. While Benn Ramon continued to impress me about New Jersey and how well they paid. So, I decided to go over there. I went to Asbury Park, New Jersey. I found a room there. I caught the train and went to Perth Amboy. That's where the federal employment agency was. Ramon had told me what to do. So I told those folks that I was a sheet metal man. But when I got to the superintendent and talk with him, he asked me where had I worked and I told him somewhere down in Mississippi. I gave a fictitious name and gave him my home address. That way if he wrote, the letter would come to my house. He talked with me and he knew I didn't

35

know anything about sheet metal. So he said, "I'll give you a job but I can't send you to the sheet metal shop."

Well I had to have a job because I was getting ready to go back to school. I wasn't going to be there long; I had to take what they gave me. He sent me on out there to the labor foreman. The labor foreman took my papers and looked at them and he said, "You a sheet metal man?"

Well I had lied, so I said, "Yes!"

So, he said, "Well, I don't know why they sent you out here. They should have sent you to the sheet metal shop since they need somebody over there." He took my papers and he took me over there. Something really strange happened. It was a fellow there that none of the workers could get along with. They called him Steve, that's all I ever knew him by. So, Steve's problem was he always wanted to be the boss of everything. That's what I found it to be. So when they sent me over there, my problem with the superintendent was there weren't any blacks there and he wasn't going to send me over there. That's really what it was. But after I got over there, they thought they could spite Steve and hired me to work with him. Of course, they did me a great favor. I got out there working with Steve and he showed me everything.

When he would give me something to do, I would get up and get it done. They were not used to that! So Steve started liking me. He took all kind of pain with me. Taught me really well how to do everything. After I was there a week, Steve went on his vacation. When he went on his vacation, the superintendent was around there trying to find somebody to come over there to build the elbow that Steve and I were building. Each man that they talked with would say that he couldn't do it. He happened to come by me.

Somebody had told me what he was looking for. I said

to him, "You looking for somebody to build the elbow? I can do that!"

He said, "Now, how are you going to build an elbow and you have only been here a week? These men been here ten years and they can't do it!"

I said, "Well, I don't have anything do with them being here ten years. I'm just telling you what I can do."

So after they couldn't find anybody, they sent Bob, a middle-aged white man, over to me and he told me right off, he said, "I don't know a thing I can do over here. The superintendent told me to come over here and I'm going to be your helper and do whatever you say."

I was the boss. We worked together and we got things out just like Steve had been doing. When my shift was over at just about six o'clock that morning, the superintendent was up there and I asked him to come and check it because we were about ready to put it out. He came in to check it and he said, "Well, I can't see nothing particularly wrong with it. So, if it doesn't fit, they will put it back out at the door and we will have to figure out something else to do."

Well I got through with it and put it out. During that time I was riding up to Perth Amboy with Charlie. Charlie would always be late going to work; he was in a hurry. I was afraid he was going to have a wreck. That's why I went on up there and found me a room and I was able to work in O'Keff coal yard. When I would get in the first thing in the morning I would work a while then I would go to bed and rest until it was time for me to go to work in the shipyard. And that's what I did to make extra money. While I was doing that Charlie was a welder. He taught me how to weld. I learned to weld but I didn't keep up with it, but I was a good welder. I did weld some of the parts of the ship back there when I would have spare time

37

waiting to get something done. I would weld on our part but it was something he taught me how to do. I stayed on there and made that elbow. I came in that next day early about four o'clock to see if that elbow was used or at the door. It was not lying around in there. I went down to the ships that were in the harbor. I couldn't find it on them. So, I came back; I was satisfied. Then I went under the shed where they kept lumber and nobody could see me. It was about four thirty or five o'clock. The superintendent came in and he was looking. So, he couldn't find it. When the time came for me to go to work, he was standing outside the door.

I said, "You want me to continue to make it?"

He said, "Well, I guess so. I don't see it and I can't find it. This is what we will do; we will make it until they stop us." I made that elbow until Steve came back. They never did turn one of them down.

That gave me the knowledge that I was real good in shop work. I had worked in the wood shop and the change from wood to steel was no big deal. That's why it was so easy for me to fit in. I stayed up there until it was time for me to go to school. I told them I was going back to school because they were encouraging me to go back to school. And I did. But they told me if I ever needed a job to come back. My job would always be open. But I never did go back.

Four

Now when I got back to school that fall, I had some money and I was well-dressed. My sister had gone and I had to find a place to live. I got a room with Mrs. Young. She stayed close to the school in a big house. She would rent those rooms to us boys to go to school. The rent wasn't much. She would charge us a dollar and a quarter a week. It so happened, that I had gotten a job at Stine's Store. It was a dry goods store. I would sweep the floor up every morning. I would wash the windows on Fridays or Saturdays, I believe. That was one way I paid my rent. I was eating off about seventy-five cents a week. People could hardly believe that but that was all I would eat. I would eat one meal a day. Maybe sometimes I would buy some peas and cook some of them. You could get a whole lot of peas for a dime and they would last you all week. That's the way I did it as long as I was in school.

I went to school with some of the boys that were drafted into the army. I believe it was the Chrysler boys, or one of them. That left a janitorial position open. The school did not pay much so this was a way of keeping the school clean. I got that job with the school which paid six dollars a month. I didn't change my living style at all.

When school was out I was always able to find work somewhere. But in the meantime, I was able to buy some clothes. Emmit Field was making suits for young men at that time. He made a suit for me. I bought a nice suit and

I was pretty well dressed then. I was able to compete with those city boys. This is where I ran into John Dancy Woodard. He had a car and, incidentally, he was real popular. His auntie was married to the undertaker there. He and I became so close until I started staying up there sometimes with him at the undertakers. I would go with him to pick up bodies. From then on he and I became even closer. Before he finished school, that next year when we got out, we were supposed to go to Navico, Alabama. It was a big mill over there and we were going to get a job.

I had served in the navy and he hadn't. He had his registration card. When school was out we decided to go to Navico, Alabama. I think he was a junior. We got to Gulf Port on our way to Mobile because he had been down there before. The police stopped us. In those days, every time a bus came to a station, a whole bunch of police would always meet the bus. He came up like they always do. They would check the black boys' credentials. I happened to have that paper that they had given me when I went to the navy. John had his registration card and he was all right.

When he got to me, he said, "This isn't any good. We're going to take you to jail."

John said, "Well, sir if you gone take him, take me too because we are together."

Well, then I had a chance to think. I said, "Officer, I was discharged from the navy. If you don't believe me you call Madison County Chancery Officer and tell them to look in book two and page forty-three and you'll find my discharge has been recorded in that book." Then he finally let us go. We decided to come on back home.

I came back and my brother was in Milwaukee so I went up there. I got a job at Firestone Steel. I worked there that summer. And that time in Milwaukee they had a gymnasium where young boys go and work out to be boxers. I was already noted for being a good puncher, which was boxing. I could hit real hard. I bought some gloves and got my training gear and started training. I didn't know you'd have to fight amateur for so long before you could fight professionally. Had I known that I probably would have still been up there. While I was in there, I would be training and the other boys would see me hitting the punching bag and none of the amateurs would get in the ring with me. They said I hit too hard. The only time I got a chance to get a little experience was when I got in the ring with a professional.

Aside from that, I wasn't happy with the place I was rooming so I found another place. I was with a lady called Willie Calhoun. And while I was there I worked at night. If it was something better out there I could use the daytime to find it. That's why I chose to work at night all the time. Plus the fact you would get a bonus of ten percent. But while I was there it was another lady; she was a beautiful black woman! Wooo! I never seen one with skin as pretty as hers! I decided I was gonna approach her and I did. And of course, she embarrassed me. She told me she had a daughter as old as I was and she was too old for me. So the woman shamed me out so bad until I was ashamed to meet her. For a long time, I dodged her. I wouldn't be around her even though we were staying in the same house. I could always find a way not to meet her.

I would always pay my rent on time. I went back to school. Willie told me before I left there that if I stayed there and went into the fight ring I could make more money than I would ever make on a regular job. She was right but I didn't have sense enough to understand it and I didn't trust her. I thought that her motive was to have me there because I paid rent good. So, I left and went back to school.

I was in the eleventh grade that year. I went back to work for the school. At that time, I had moved up some. The boy that was working for Logan Gross had gone to the army. I was fortunate to get that job. I went to work there and I was still able to work at the school. Everything was really working well for me. I had chance to work for the Seal Lily Ice Cream Store on the weekends. I would deliver ice cream on a bicycle all over town. At that time, we had those bricks of ice cream and people called in for them. I would deliver it to the houses all over town. I can recall how my boss always said that nobody could steal from him. Every night after work he was always bragging about how he had caught some of his other employees trying to steal his ice cream by hiding it in a garbage can in the back of the building. After work, they would go back there and get it. However, he caught on to it and busted them. He was always going on about how you could not steal his ice cream from him because it was impossible. I would just stand there laughing at him because I would have a brick of ice cream under each of my arms beneath my coat! I just had to prove that I could steal from him and not get caught! I didn't want the ice cream. I would always give it to someone out on the street. I just had a point to make.

So, that job really helped me to dress well. I was able to compete with the city boys. Most of them had little jobs. I had some nice clothes and that's how I was able to take some of the big shot girls to the show. That was the biggest thing that we had at that time.

I remember taking Dot Carter out. Dot Carter's daddy was a railroad worker. Those were the kind of jobs that black people had at that time that were considered big shots. Some of them even had a chance to carry mail. They would always have a good income coming in. So I was really popular. After that, I think it was Mary Galloway. I got friendly with her. She and her sister were going to school. Dot was ahead of me anyway and she finished school and went on to college. I don't know where she went but when I knew anything she had married the man that became president of Alcorn College, Dr. Washington.

Well, I was going to see Mary and she lived out near the Natchez Trace. In fact, the Galloways live out there now. Her daddy knew my daddy they were really good friends. She and I got alone really well. But she was ahead of me, also. She finished high school and went to Jackson State. Of course, I hadn't finished school at that time. I didn't keep in contact with her. When I did finish high school the following year I went to Rust College.

I finished the next year in school; I was able then to travel. I went back to Milwaukee and to the same people. I found a job there. I had been trying to get on at A.O. Smith where my brother worked. They were really hiring there and making good money. That was during the wartime. I got there and the war ended in forty-five. It had to have been in forty-five because I finished school the next year. I was a senior the next year. I couldn't work at Firestone because they were not hiring anybody. I started to working for Cutler and Hammer. I met a white fellow there; his name was Carl. They were plating electrical parts. They were the same thing that you see and use in your house, electrical boxes that hold wires. Some of it looked like copper. That was the kind of work we were doing. Carl found out I had been training to be a boxer and he wanted me to stay there. He wanted to be my manager. Well, I didn't get into it because I knew I wasn't going to be there long. I was going back to school.

That year I went home. That's the year Mr. Clifton Goodloe began bringing cars from Detroit and selling them down here in Mississippi. I bought one. I think I paid six hundred for a '36 Plymouth. At that time during the war they had stopped making cars. It was really hard to get a car. I was really glad to get such a good car considering how difficult it was to get one. They started to making cars again in '46 or '47 once the war was over. It was a good car! It was hit by a train. I was traveling in south Canton going up a hill. At the top of the hill was a train track. My car stalled on the train tracks and a train was coming. I saw the lights and stepped out of the car. My car was completely demolished.

I was staying at home and driving to school every day. My other brothers were riding to school with me. That's the year that I graduated from high school. Of course, I worked in Milwaukee that summer. Well, before I graduated, I was traveling around town, popular with the girls. That was during the school year. So, that's about the time I ran into a girl named Louise Nash. I was headed home and she was walking home. I would always pick up people. At that time it wasn't a whole lot of cars and people would let you ride. I let her ride. I asked her where she was going. She told me where she was headed and I told her I was going that way and I would drop her off at home. I got acquainted with her and we started going out together.

We kept going out together at that point, and, of course, accidentally she got pregnant. That was my senior year in high school. And she would call down to the school because I didn't have a telephone and she couldn't reach me otherwise. Mrs. Rodgers was the dominant factor at school and she told me the girl called. She didn't tell me to work with the girl and take my responsibility and be a man. She was discouraging me, telling me, "These old girls get out here and get pregnant by a married man and then they want to put it on these single boys. You stay away from out there; come on to school and finish your work here." And that's what I did because I had a good reputation in school. In fact, Mrs. Rodgers was lord and God. Whatever she said, that was it and nobody challenged it. I guess I was no exception. I did just what she said. In that I learned this one thing. I would think about that after I was gone and I became more concerned with each passing day. And really for a long while that bothered me so much that I couldn't hardly set down by myself without thinking about it. I think now if a young man is not informed correctly and he doesn't do the right thing, he will regret it the rest of his life. And I regret that right today. She told me to do that.

So when I graduated that year, I worked across the summer. I decided to go to Rust College because that's where Professor Rodgers went. He encouraged us all to go there. He didn't encourage us to go to just any college. He was more concerned about us going to Rust because that's where he went. That's what most of those old principals did at that time. Whatever college they graduated from, that's where they wanted their former students to attend. As I grew older I could understand this concept because everybody was always trying to support his or her alma mater. That's why he encouraged me to go to Rust College. While I was there, Dr. McCoy gave me a job. The first thing I had to do was to milk the cows. I was used to that, coming from the farm like I did. I had been milking cows when I was at home. Two more fellows, the Hayes brothers, they were twins, and I were staying in a house right back of the campus. We got along really well. We were all working for the school and things just worked out well for them, and me also.

I came home that December. My distant cousin, Dr. Davis, president of Tennessee State, he and Mother recognized one another. I ran upon him. I guess somebody had told him about me or maybe Mother told him because they talked occasionally. He encouraged me to go to Tennessee State. I left Rust and went on up there. When I got there, I didn't like it there. He gave me a job just like he said. But the thing about it was all the boys were veterans. It was a lot of veterans there. Those that were not veterans had parents that were able to support them. They had a good football team at that time. All the boys were wanting to go there. They had a good swimming team.

They had many things that we didn't have at Rust. The thing about Rust was I was more familiar with the way things were done and they treated me better. The environment was better for me. Up there, those boys either were veterans and were drawing money every month or their parents were able to help them. I went with my friend, James Goodloe. He took me up there and brought me back when I came back. The thing that got me with James was when we got ready to go he said, "McCullough, we gone get ready to go home. You want to go?"

I said, "Well, Goodloe, I'd like to go but I don't have any money."

He said, "You don't have to have any money. You come and ride with me." He had a new car and he was a veteran, too. I decided not to return to Tennessee State because those boys were able to have big times on the weekends. They would buy wine and dine out and go round there and I couldn't do it. I just felt out of place. Therefore, I just went on back to Rust.

When I went back to Rust I got my old job back. I worked and went to school. They had summer school and I was able to make up the time that I lost when I went to Tennessee State. From there on out, I remained a permanent fixture at Rust. I started picking up mail and different things like that. Eventually, I started raising chickens for the school. I stopped milking cows and took on the job of raising chickens. I really enjoyed the job. I started gathering eggs. They didn't have to tell me to. I would clean out the chicken houses and get everything ready. Then when the chickens were large enough, we had to kill and pick them. That was the first time I had seen a picker. The school had one. We picked the chicks, gutted them and carried them to Red Bank and put them in a freezer. I got real good at that.

I happened to make one mistake. I got back there during spring training. I went to observe the football training. I didn't know a thing about football because we didn't have it down here in Canton. I began bragging and talking about how sorry the boys were and what I could do if I was playing. I fooled around and the time came one day when they were training and the coach asked me about coming out there and practicing. So, I went out there with my smart self. This is what happened. It was an old boy there from Dallas, Texas, Oscar Hathawell. He played center for the team. He was a good center. They got me in front of him and I tell you the truth, before I started good, I sprung both of my ankles in almost the same hour!

When I left that football field I couldn't limp on one leg for the other one! I got over that, and of course, when I came back that fall I had gotten hold of a book put out by Quaker Oats. I read up on it and it had Doak Walker's picture on it. He was a big star at that time at Southern

Methodist. I was encouraged by William McDougal. He played football where he went to school. I think he played some in the army, too. He was good. So he was teaching me how to do. I was really prepared. That summer I found out how far they would have to run.

Five

Rodger McMillan and Charles Cole weighed about 240 pounds apiece. They were the two on me. One of them was supposed to hit me high and the other was to hit me low. That was how you were supposed to move a man out like that. But I was too swift for them and too strong. At that time you could hit a man on his helmet with the open part of your hand. I hit him with the back part of my hand and I jabbed him so hard that it stunned him a little while. I would stop one of them and would pass right by the other one while he was trying to come back to. I did that about three or four times. Then the boys began to joke about me running through two men!

The next time I went through them, McMillan caught my leg. He caught my leg when I was going through and made me fall. And when I fell, my knee fell on his ankle and broke his ankle. Therefore, from then on I had to play in his position. But what they didn't know was that I had learned all the things that I needed to do to get in condition. When they came back that fall and started practicing, I was already in shape. That's one of the things that gave me the advantage over them. I already had this good training and was just really prepared for it. That year I played.

I stayed around the campus all the summer. Another advantage it gave me, my job was to meet all of the ladies and to help them put their trunks or suitcases up in their rooms in the dormitories. If they had heavy trunks or luggage it was my job to help them get it in their rooms. That was an advantage given to me. I would be able to see all the new girls coming in and tell the boys about them. I would tell them who was the best looking girl coming in. Well, I was the judge and I was a good judge. If I told them that this girl was the best looking on campus you would find that every boy agreed with me because I could really judge the most beautiful lady. So every boy wanted to see her because I was a good judge.

While being there on the campus that summer and having to play football that fall, I practiced and got in really good shape. I really played well that year. In fact, I played so well everybody was really surprised at me, not having any experience on the football field and coming out and doing so well that first year.

That rocked on, and I never thought much about it. When the next year came up, that's the year we went down to play Alcorn and they had that game in Meridian. Alcorn was really high rated that year. We got down and we were all in the hotel where black boys would stay. The Alcorn boys came in making a lot of noise. We were quiet. Our quarterback was David Self. Self said, "That's ole big mouth Charles Evers making all of that noise." It never dawned on me who Charles was. When I came to think about Charles again was when he came back from Chicago to take his brother's place over the NAACP. That's when I really associated the name Charles Evers with that football team.

During that game they had a big 'ole boy on that team. He weighed a whole lot more than I did. He weighed nearly three hundred pounds. His name was Thomas and his number was 50. I never will forget that. I was handling those boys and getting through them so

50

well they had to put three men on me. They had two men on me. Then they had to have another one on me to help block me, otherwise the play wouldn't go. Finally somehow or another, I got hit someway and fell. Thomas fell on me with his knee! His knee hit me in my side and I tell you I saw every star in the heaven. I was just knocked out. But I still played. I guess I had established myself to be unstoppable until they had such great respect for me until they didn't know I was hurt. If they had they probably would have killed me. I played on and at the half I didn't know my way off the field. Somebody had to get me off the field. Then when we got ready for the second half, well we got to talking, the coach got to talking to some of those boys telling about how I was hurting. He said, "Yeah, but McCullough do better hurt than you fellows do when you are not hurt. I'm gone let him go back out there." Alcorn was supposed to beat us about three touchdowns. We wound up with a tie. I believe it was 6 to 6! Our kicker missed our extra point and their kicker missed their extra point. And that's the way the game ended. When we came off of that field that night, that's the first time I had heard that record about "Saturday Night Fish Fry." Everybody was having so much fun. Of course, our team was really fired up because we didn't lose the game. They were having all kinds of fun off of that song. I was hurting so bad I couldn't have fun off of nothing. But I remember that. When I did get through I was really able to enjoy it. From there that year I made all conference as a tackle. Then they really had respect for me all over the conference.

Meantime my work on the campus . . . What happened one day I was carrying the key back in the house for the station wagon. I ran into President McCall's daughter, Miss Hillder. I told her, I said, "Miss Hillder, your car need washing." She had a Packard. At that time it was a really popular car. It was a big car.

She said, "Well, it does need washing bad."

I told her, "Well, if you leave it parked at the hydrant next time you drive it and I'll wash it for you." And I started walking out the door.

She said, "I'll tell you what, the key is gone be here. If you ever have time, just come on in here and get the key and go on out there and wash it." So then I took the time and got her key, washed and cleaned her car up. Had it looking good for her.

So, her job was most of the time to go get the celebrity of the Methodist Conference such as Dr. Matthew S. Davage and others. I remember Dr. Davage because one day she asked me if I had my driver's license. And I told her yes. And she asked, "Would you drive Dr. Davage to Memphis for me?" And I told her, "I sure will." So I did. I took Dr. Davage to Memphis for her. You know it wasn't many cars at that time. And I guess Dr. Davage told her how careful I was. Something had to have happened because when I saw her again, I didn't see her every day, she told me, "This key is gone be right here. Any time you want to use this car the key will be here." That gave me the chance to have the use of an automobile. I wasn't abusive, I only used it across the summer when the in-service teachers came in and I would be there to ride around with them. That would be the only time I would try to use the car. I tell people that little things mean a lot. I didn't do a thing but wash that car, about an hour, hour and a half work. And therefore, I was able to use it any time I wanted. It really taught me a lesson, that's what really happened. You do little things not expecting your reward to be so great.

After I got to be a star on the football team; that was

another thing I was doing. I was going to get the mail in the station wagon for the school. Then it came up about me being a star and Tom Doxie came to Holly Springs. I guess that was his home originally, but he had been in the army. He and his wife came in there and opened up a cleaners. I don't know who sent him, but he came to me, and asked me to pick up the clothes on the campus for him and bring them to his cleaners. So I agreed to do that. He was gone pay me so much to do it. So, I did. Because all the students on the campus had great admiration for me then I had all the time on hand. McDougal and Roy Miles, when they would buy paper every month, they were veterans and they would always buy paper for me. So you can see, I had real good relations with all on the campus. So it wasn't any problem for me to get their clothes. That saved them from having to walk up to the cleaners. That helped me out, too. I did so well that Tom decided he would buy a panel truck and he wanted me to pick up in the city and I did. I picked up out in the city and did well out there. That really helped me financially to be on campus like I was. I really enjoyed my good relations with Tom.

So I worked with him until I finished school up there. Then he offered to give me half interest in his business if I would stay there and work with him. I didn't have sense enough to take it. I was out looking for a job and I had a great opportunity right there.

Before I left there across the summer I had met a girl when I was a junior. Her name was Dorothy Smith. She and I got to be real close. She was telling me she had a boyfriend at home. I never thought about him being home. I was thinking about while she was here. She told me when he was coming to see her. But it ran on a long time after that. I forgot when she told me when her boyfriend was gone come to see her. At that time, generally, boys would go see girls on Wednesday nights. And that's what I did. But before I went, I had a friend stay over there by me. He was off campus, too. We called him Sug. He would talk with me. He said, "McCullough, that's such a pretty girl. You ought to marry that girl." He really persuaded me to go. So, I went to ask her to marry me.

Another boy was there and his name was Samuel Robinson. He was working on campus. I told Samuel when he got through with the station wagon (it was a new station wagon, they had three station wagons. Miss Doxie used them most on singing tours). I told Sammy to fill the station wagon up with gas. And he did. When night came I got off work, I got dressed, went and stole the station wagon and drove up to Ripley. The girl didn't really live in Ripley. She lived in the country. When I got there and found out where she lived, she and I were talking and her boyfriend came up. I really was gone ask her about marriage. When he came I didn't get the chance to pop the question to her. She said, "Well, you know what we agreed on. This is that time. He is coming in. You know we agreed that I would never confront you in front of your girlfriend and you agreed the same." So, that really hurt me. I had to leave. I never did go see Dorothy anymore.

In '49, I finished in December of that year and I played ball and that's the year the school switched to the platoon system. I remember we played Jackson State up there and Jackson beat us. Really what they did they wore us down. That's the first time I heard that before. We just played the whole game. Jackson wore us down in the third quarter and they went on and beat us pretty bad. That's the last game I played on Rust campus.

I finished but I had to come back that spring to march. I left there and I went to New Orleans to get a job and I did get one at Borden's Milk Co. But, you know, it wasn't nothing then but labor, that's all, and I didn't like that. I came back home and while I was there, some boys came in here from Detroit. I met them over at the night-club, Hamlin's Nightclub. They were popping off telling us, and you know boys exaggerate when they come in here with new cars. They didn't have anything else but the new cars. It was so impressive when they came down here like that. And they were telling me if I come up there I could get a job. I had an idea that if I could get in with a car company I could make a steel-top convertible. That was in '49 or '50. And of course, Ford came out with that top in 1957. If I could have gotten in there, see I would have had an opportunity to present that to Ford. But I went to Detroit and stayed with my cousin, Garfield Heath. I didn't have any money amount to anything. I told him and he said well you don't have to have money just wait until you work. If you get some money, give me something, if you don't, it's all right.

I went to the automobile factories. In fact, he took me to all of them. He took me to Chrysler first, but they weren't hiring. Then he took me to Chevrolet. They weren't hiring. He took me to Ford. They weren't hiring. So, he told me, "Well, just wait and we will go next week."

We waited and went back the next week. He took me back to the Chrysler place; they were not hiring. Then he took me to the Chevrolet place and they were hiring every other man. There were about fifty or seventy-five of us in line and they hired the man in front of me and the man behind me. I was really disappointed. I went back the next time to Ford. Ford had about fifty or seventy-five men ahead of me. I don't remember the exact number, but it was in that number. They hired fifty men right up to me and they cut off. And I just felt like Detroit was a bad luck place to me. I had to leave Detroit.

Then, I went to Racine, Wisconsin. I went to the Nash Plant to try to get a job there. I did not get the job there. The folks were cutting up and carrying on and acting so silly. But you know what, every one of those acting a fool got hired. There I was acting dignified and it didn't matter. I went back to Milwaukee. I went to the bank where I had my little money and I wanted to buy some stock. I always wanted to buy stock, but at that time, the bank wouldn't buy stock for black people. I didn't know that. I thought when I was up North I would be able to get anything I wanted. But I found out that I couldn't. The man told me, "The little money you have . . . you better keep it." So, I took the money out of the bank and went and bought a car and came home. That was in December.

So, I got here. I happened to run into Ms. Velma Jackson. She was the Jean Supervisor. She was the assistant superintendent, but they didn't give her that title. She hired me and sent me out to Farmhaven and I worked out there until school was out. Of course, she wanted me to stay there and she was promising a lot, which she did do. She wasn't misleading me. I happened to run into Professor Rogers. He asked me to come back and teach at Cameron Street and that was my alma mater and I guess every graduate in the country would be happy to go back and teach at his or her alma mater whether it is high school or college.

So that's what I did. I went there and I taught there for two years. During the last year, they started a federal program where they were teaching veterans. That was right when a big bunch of veterans were getting out of the army and they were training them and helping them to get back adjusted to civilian life. I was working in that program and the thing that really got next to me was how long it took the government to pay. I was not used to that. I didn't know that the government would drag around that way paying folks.

So I needed some tires on my car. I had bought me a good car. In fact, I had bought two. The first one I bought was a 1947 Pontiac. It was a good-looking car. And my brother wrecked it. I bought another Pontiac and I didn't realize it, but it had been wrecked. But with my limited experience with cars, I didn't know it. So, when I discovered that it had been wrecked, the frame was cracked and I decided it was to dangerous to drive. I didn't have the credit and I needed some tires on it. So, since they were not lending too much money at that time to black people, I had a little trouble getting tires. I decided to go ahead and trade the car. It was easier to trade a car and get one with tires on it than it was to buy tires from a tire dealer.

So, I did trade that car for a 1950 Catalina. Of course, when I did that and school was out that year, I decided that I wasn't going to teach anymore and I was leaving and I didn't want to be bothered with federal payroll. That was a mistake, but all things don't work like that. At that time, I was so disgusted with the way they had handled the payroll that I just decided I didn't want to work for the government anymore.

So, then I decided to go to Chicago. And I did. I went to Chicago and I had a friend up there. His name was Willie Goodloe. We were friends while we were in high school here in Canton. He had been up there and he was familiar with the city. I got in touch with him through his mother. He took me around and got me a room. Of course, at that time a room was plentiful and you didn't have a whole lot of thugs in Chicago like they have now. A man could just about get a room anywhere.

So then, that's when I went to look for work. I got there that Sunday evening and went to the room and settled in. Then I bought me a newspaper. And while looking in the newspaper I saw where they wanted a recent graduate, which I was. I had been out of school two years. They wanted someone who majored in math and minored in chemistry. And I had that. And I was so happy to find that kind of job advertised. I just knew I was going be the one to get it. But I didn't realize even though at the time I was in the North I couldn't get that kind of job. I was thinking that when you get up North, things would be different from the South. Had I been in the South, I would have known that they were not talking about blacks. But it was the same thing up there. So, I rushed out that Monday morning and went to Western Electric. They interviewed me and I was still feeling pretty good. But I was suspicious because of how things were going. So, the last thing he asked me. "Do you have your birth certificate?"

I got kind of lit up a little then because I thought I was going get the job. And I said, "Yes, but I don't have it with me. It is at the house. I can go get it."

He said, "Well, go get it."

So, I left in a hurry and went back to the house and got my birth certificate and I came back. I didn't see that man. I ran into somebody else. And of course, he didn't hire me. He didn't tell me he wasn't going to hire me. But he just kept fooling around and I knew it was something wrong. They kept just giving me the run around until I just decided to leave. So I left there and went somewhere else looking.

During that time, there were signs up: HELP WANTED all over the city. So, I wound up going across to a place called Mallory Steel. That was in Cicero. Blacks didn't live out in that area at that time. So, I went out there and got hired at Mallory Steel. I worked there for a while. Of course, other boys were talking about the salaries they were getting and I became dissatisfied with my salary. So, I went riding around the city.

I met a classmate of mine, S.T. Nero. I was just driving around the city and ran into him. We stopped and chatted and exchanged addresses. He told me to come by and holler at him sometimes and I did. So, I went one day to his house. I found out that he was working with the post office. Of course, he told me to be sure to put an application in to try to get on at the post office. Well, it was paying much better than where I was working, so I was really concerned about that. So I did. He told me to go in and put in an application in either October or November. I did that and got hired. Of course, I was hired as part-time worker in the post office. On my other job I was working ten hours a day. But, on the weekend, I put in sometimes thirteen or fourteen hours a day at the post office. I remember Saturday night I put in long hours like that and I came from work that Sunday and I got to a red light and went to sleep. Everybody was blowing and going and I woke up and went on to the house. I got in the bathtub and I went to sleep in the bathtub.

So, I think I overcame that and I stayed there and got some sleep. Then I was ready to go back to work. I worked like that for three months. Most of the people who got hired in the post office work like that. So, while I was there I met a middle-aged lady. At that time she told me, "Why don't you try to get a permanent position with the post office?" She said it was because they do have depressions from time to time in this country and the post office is one that never lays off. So, I decided I was going to try that. Of course, I did everything I could to make sure that

59

my work was pleasing to my supervisor, but something happened. At least I did something.

There was an old lady who came in there working part-time, too, and my sympathy was for her. We were standing up. I was young. I was about twenty-nine. So, she came in there. I am pretty sure that lady was in her late sixties. She was trying to stand and she looked like she was having such a hard time. Then I decided to go over in the New York letter section and get a stool from there and give it to her, and I did. I was working in the Michigan letter section right next to it and that's where I found a vacant stool there and I brought it over to her. I didn't worry about one for myself. But, that foreman in New York section was the one who kept me from getting hired at the post office. He told my foreman not to recommend me when the time comes after the holidays are over. He didn't want him to hire me because he said I came over there and stole a stool out of the New York letter section. That kept me from getting a job at the post office. I was really sorry about that.

However, I worked there and this job wasn't getting better. I started going from one job to another. Finally, I went out there and I was looking and I saw a rubber plant. I decided I wanted to go to work for a rubber plant. At that time, I had an idea about building a puncture-proof tire. That's why I wanted to get into a rubber plant. The rubber plant and Westinghouse were pretty close together. The way you come in, you got to the Westinghouse first. I wasn't paying too much attention. I just walked in it. When I picked up the application, I realized then that it was not where I wanted to be. But I said, "Well, since I'm in here, I'm going to fill out this application." I filled it out and they hired me.

After they hired me, I didn't want to be off of work.

You know, when you're off like that, you need to be bringing in an income all the time, so I decided to go on and
work there. I stayed there. That was during Eisenhower's
years. I think the election was coming up and work had
gotten slow and they were telling us that after the election was over we would probably go back fulltime because
we would be getting government contracts. So, I got laid
off. After I got laid off there, I started working with little
jobs, one after another. I wasn't happy with any of them.

That's when I was introduced to policy. Now, I had
been rooming with this lady Rosie. She played policy and
a pick up boy comes to your house and gets your numbers
and takes them into their headquarters. So, I had just
been watching the numbers every night and really I had
gotten where I could pick them out good. I remember that
Saturday night she caught about $60.00 and she said,
"Jesse, don't you want to play?" She encouraged me to
play and she gave me $5.00 to play with. I went on and
wrote up the numbers and of course by me studying the
numbers like I had and had been dealing with it in college
really about permutation combinations. I had myself organized pretty good. The first day I played that morning
(that was on a Saturday evening when she told me to
play). I picked out the numbers and gave them to her and
she sent them in that Monday. When I came back from
work, I had caught $10.00. Then, I played that back that
night and caught $15.00.

I really started playing numbers and it didn't take
long for me to become a policy addict. I would be out and
driving my car and I would see numbers on door signs and
doors where people have their numbers up and whatever
number would come to my mind like that, I would come
back and play it. I did that for a month. Then, I could just
be walking down the street and I could see numbers in

the air and I would come back and play them. Then, I began winning every time I played. I did that for over a month or better. I was catching so regular (I caught twice every day, every time they played). I really thought I knew what I was doing. Well, I did have a little idea.

I decided that I was going to really play heavy one Friday night. I wasn't going to have to go to work. I told Booker, the pick up boy, I wanted to go and pull. He said, "Alright." They would be glad for me to come there and pull. So, I went and pulled that night and I loaded my number up. I said since I was going to be pulling, I'm going to just play heavy. That's when I found out that I wasn't that good. I didn't catch anything and that changed my perception about playing policy. I did learn.

After that, I started working on another scheme. Of course, that scheme worked for me. But, it cost a lot for me to play it. Where I was living I was playing in Rosie's book. I decided to move to another place where I could write my own book and there I started using a new system. That system cost me $250.00 a day. Of course, I didn't lose anymore playing $250.00 than I did when I was playing $5.00 because the system was so well organized and the combinations were so put together that I didn't lose anymore. So, the managers of the wheel realized that. All I needed to do was catch those first numbers and I would have every number they pulled. So, they told the pick up boy, "Don't bring that book in no more." That was the end of my policy playing.

During that time, integration was really hot. So, I decided that I was going to come back and teach in Mississippi like I had planned. I had planned when I went up there to try to make enough money to be able to take care of my family without my wife working. That was my plan. When I went up there I thought about how my mother used to work. I always said I didn't want my wife to go to the field and work like that. So, then I decided to return to Mississippi and get back in the school system. That's what I did. I came back to Mississippi. I didn't exactly leave on my own notion. I had gotten a letter telling me that Mr. Sylvester Barnes was the principal in Morton. He wanted to get in touch with me. So, I wrote him and he said he wanted me to come there and teach math. So, I decided to come on back to Mississippi and teach.

I was assistant coach and I enjoyed that. While coaching over there during the first year I was there, Morton had a pretty good team. Really, they had a good team. We won the Northern Division and Hattiesburg won in the Southern Division. We were supposed to play Greenwood. At that time, Mr. Thredguild was principal up there. They were supposed to come and play Morton. Of course, at the time they were supposed to come, Greenwood did not show up. They called our school. After it was so late and they had not come they said, "Well, we forgot." Well, what I discovered was they didn't forget. They did that intentionally because they figured if we came up there, on their home turf, they would be able to take the game. So, I persuaded Mr. Barnes not to reschedule that game.

The conference had a rule. Joe Hardy was the coach at that time. The conference said that if a team failed to come, they forfeited the game by two points. Well, those big shots who ran the conference (Thredguild, Sprig, Hawkins and Burger) were trying to maneuver Morton to accommodate Mr. Thredguild because they called all the shots at that time. But, after I was there, I was going to see that they didn't do it anymore. So, they finally had a meeting. They called a conference meeting to discuss it. When we got there, I was still trying to persuade the principal, Mr. Barnes, not to give in to them. Let's just stay like we were. We'd take the game. They didn't come and play. Let's just go ahead on and be the Northern champs. And that's what we did. Of course, we played that game in Hattiesburg and they won the game, but at least Morton had a chance to represent the Northern Division.

Mr. Thredguild talked about me saying, "Young man, you don't understand." But, I understood better than he did. I understood that it didn't make sense to let a few people dominate the conference.

I guess they were glad when I left. I didn't leave that year, but I left the next year. I liked all of the people over there in Morton and all of them seemed to like me. The reason I left was because that year, they decided to split the session for the farmers and have so many months in the summer and so many months in the fall and winter when they would go to school. I didn't like the split session. That's why I left Morton.

Before I left Morton, I met with Mr. Barnes. The principals were having a meeting in Jackson. They were having a meeting to discuss the training of teachers that they were sending out. At that time they were sending student teachers out to different schools to let them get experience in teaching. Mr. Barnes wanted me to take him over there because I had the best car. I took him over there. I met a lady, Ms. Henry, who I had worked with when I first came out of college back in 1949 or 1950. So, Ms. Henry told some of the girls there that she knew me. She knew the girls that were coming to Morton. She told them that I was her ex-boyfriend.

Of course, Ms. Henry was nearly old enough to be my mother. She didn't look good and she didn't have long hair. I didn't care nothing about her. But, she told them that we'd had a relationship. I was not married at that time so I started to go out with two of the young ladies. I started going around with them. However, I did get tied up with one. For the sake of her privacy, I will call her Betty Smith. I feel that would be a better name to use instead of her real name. That's just enough to identify with what really happened. We got really close. I used to take those two young ladies around to different places, help them to find hairdressers and things like that. Eventually, they left and I had gotten kind of close with Betty. She went back to Jackson State and I went to Chicago when school was out. Before I went back to Chicago I spent some time on Rust College campus. My plan was to leave there Sunday night about one o'clock. The reason I left at one o'clock was because the Tennessee law enforcement were so strict on out of state tags. I wanted to leave at that hour to get through Tennessee before the officers got on the road that Monday morning. While I was at Rust, I called Tom Doxey's brother and got Tom's telephone number.

I left the college and headed to Chicago. When I got in Memphis, I called Tom. He was living in West Memphis, Arkansas. He met me in Memphis and carried me to his nightclub and offered me half interest if I would stay and help him run it. I refused. So, the next time I heard from Tom, he was in Chicago, too. Before I got out of Tennessee, I was driving at the speed of 105 miles per hour. I was alone. When I got to Union, Tennessee, I slowed down but I was still speeding. I was driving 65 miles an hour in a 35 speed zone. An officer was parked somewhere and I didn't see him. He pulled me over and asked me what was my hurry. I told him I was not in a hurry, I just didn't realize that I was traveling that fast. So, he asked me for my driver's license. I gave it to him and he said, "Follow me." I knew I had big trouble. I only had eighty dollars in my pocket and I was sure I was not going to be able to get out of Union City, Tennessee. When we got to the station, we walked in and the sergeant was sitting there with his feet propped on the desk. I knew I was going to be in Tennessee a long time.

Then the sergeant asked him how did he cooperate with the arresting officer. The officer said, "He cooperated fine."

Then the sergeant said, "What would you recommend?"

The arresting officer said, "The minimum." Which was twenty dollars.

I never felt like kissing a man before but I sure felt like kissing that officer. Then I continued on my journey to Chicago. When I got to Chicago, I ran into the Doxeys again and I met his wife, Nora. She told me Tom had died. For a while I would meet her and we would go to Arlington Race Track. After meeting her several times and going to the track, I got busy looking for a job and I didn't see her anymore.

Jobs weren't plentiful then as they had been. I was moving from place to place. I ran into one of my old schoolmates and we were really good friends. He told me about his working at Ford. I tried to get on at Ford, yet I was never able to get on. So, he told me about driving cabs on the weekends. I decided I would try that once I got a steady job. That way I would learn the city.

When the little jobs I would have would play out I would look for another. I remember going to Hot Point. They had a sign up and I was just trying to get any kind of job. I wasn't too particular because the jobs I had worked on were not too good. I had heard that Hot Point was a pretty good place to work. So, I went by and put in my application at Hot Point. They called me up and looked at my application. They said, "With your education you should be in the professional office." So they sent me over to the professional office. They told me that this man was leaving. The employment office told me to apply for that job and that's what I did. I went over there and got an application and applied for it.

When I got to the office, the man interviewed me and told me what they expected of me. Really, he was going to give me a position as bartender. I didn't mind that at all. Then my job would be to go to the airport and meeting the dignitaries that would be coming in; taking the big shots to the bank and things like that. Well, I figured that would suit me fine. So, I didn't get that job. What he told me was that I didn't know the city. I got turned down not because I didn't know the city but because I was black. They were not going to hire a black for that position. I know what happened now, but at that time I didn't realize.

In the meantime, my friends were telling me about getting the car inspected and what I would have to do to get it inspected. They informed me that you couldn't get your car inspected until you paid the folk there two dollars. But I decided that I was not going to do that. What I did, I drove down to the inspection station and before I got there I dismantled the backlights by unplugging the lights. I knew that was one of the things that they would turn you down on. He inspected everything and he told me, "Your back lights are not working." I said, "Anything else wrong?" He said, "No, that's all." So, I pulled out of there and went around and plugged up my lights, came back through and he put the sticker on. So, I didn't have to pay him anything.

Same thing happened when I went to get my driver's license. When I was getting my license exchanged they told me I would have to pay that policeman off. I decided I was not going to do that! I had been driving under a Mississippi license. I took my written test and I passed that all right. Then I had to take my road test. When I got in the car the police got in along with me. He told me to go ahead on out into the street, which was wrong. He did this so that he would have something to keep me from getting my license. I told him, "This is my car and I can't afford to drive out and let somebody tear it up. You are not going to pay for it." So, I guess he realized that I wasn't just the ordinary person. When we got back from the road test he went on and passed me and I didn't have any trouble.

Directly after that I went to work for the Checkered Cab Company. My friend, John Dancy Woodard, had persuaded me to do that. I started working for them part time. I stayed with the cab company two years. I learned the city and started going all over the city. At that time when I started driving for the cab company, the fellows that were working with the cab company would always inform me that when we were in a line somewhere at a taxi stand we would line up according to who came first. If you were three or four behind you would just get out of your cab and get in the cab in front and talk with them until one of the cabs moved up. They told me to always keep two dollars on the seat next to me because if the police stopped you then you would give him two dollars and he would let you go. Police were bad about stopping cab drivers and truck drivers because they knew that they had to have a driver's license. I kept two dollars in my pocket.

From then on I continued to drive the cab. A problem came up with the cab. I remember one day I came in on Roosevelt Road. I was headed west and an officer was headed east. We both stopped at the same light. When the light changed I pulled off. He went over there and turned around and came back behind me and said that I ran the light. I gave him two dollars. Then later on, I was on Blue Island and Cottage Grove. I was crossing Cottage Grove; I remember that. I pulled up to the pedestrian line and stopped right at the line. It wasn't over in there where it could interfere with pedestrians. The light changed and I pulled off. This policeman was on Cottage Grove and he made a left turn and came out there and stopped me. He said I ran the light. Well I decided to go ahead and give him two dollars. But then the two dollars was getting so bad, I decided I couldn't live that way. I made up my mind that I wasn't going to pay that anymore.

Fortunately for me, I was driving one night. I was at Ambassador East Hotel. I picked up a load of gentlemen to take out south. I don't remember which hotel it was, but I was carrying them out there somewhere. They were telling me where to go. We kept our park lights on at all times and the light on the top of the cab would go off when your passengers got in and you turned the meter on. Just as I pulled off, I guess I got about fifteen yards, and the police stopped me. I wondered what he wanted.

He said, "You were driving without your lights on." I had just pulled off.

My passenger in the back told me to take the ticket. Well, some of the older drivers had been telling me that if it was a big shot in the cab sometimes, they would pay the ticket for you. When he told me to take the ticket, I figured then that he was going to pay for it.

When the police left, this gentleman in the back told me, "Let me see the ticket." I handed it to him; I just knew he was going to pay it then.

He said, "I'm Judge Shawasky. Now, the police did

wrong. He should have told you to put your lights on, but he didn't do that. You hadn't pulled off far enough for him to give you a ticket. So when you come to court you come to me and I will take care of it." That's what I did. When time came for me to go to court I went in and asked for Judge Shawasky. They sent me in to his court. I made myself known to him and he dismissed the case.

While I was there I saw a lawyer in court and he had a ticket that some police had given him up north. He was defending himself. I sat there and listened to him and observed how he defended himself so I would know how to approach the bench if I ever got another ticket.

After that I left and continued to drive cabs. When I got the next ticket, I carried it to Judge Shawasky. He threw it out because he knew that they give cab drivers a bad deal. Then I was up on that same street that the lawyer who was defending himself had gotten a ticket. It was a long five-point intersection. When I got there the light was green, it turned yellow just as I got halfway under the light. I got through there and the police stopped me and gave me a ticket. I took that back to Judge Shawasky and I presented it to him. He dismissed it. I had gotten to the place that I could defend myself in court, therefore, I didn't even worry about tickets any more. I never did give anybody else two dollars not to give me a ticket.

When you are driving a cab you meet a lot of folks and you have some weird experiences. I remember picking up another man from up north somewhere. He wanted to go out south to a hotel. Well, he ended up out on Blue Island. There he told me to hold the meter. I was used to doing that because people run in to get something and they would come back to the cab continue on the trip. But this gentleman went in the hotel and told me to hold the meter. Well, I was holding the meter for so long and he didn't come back that I decided that something was wrong. I got suspicious so I decided to go in the hotel. Just as I got in there, he was heading toward the elevator. I didn't say a word to him. He had a nice watch on his arm, so I just reached out and caught his arm and snatched the watch off! I walked on out and he followed me because he wanted to get that watch. I told him, "If you want it, come and pay your bill and I'll give you your watch!" So, he paid his taxi bill and I gave him his watch.

In the meantime, while I was driving taxis, I had learned the city pretty good. It was a night club on Clarks Street called Ivanhoe. It was after two o'clock when I stopped by that place. I picked up three ladies and I took them home. The manager of the cab company always told us to always walk the ladies home or to the door to make sure they were in before I leave. I carried those three ladies to their apartment. Then they had to go back so far off the street, I was afraid someone would try to rob me there. You have all kinds of people in a city like that. Before I got out of the cab, I placed my billfold underneath the cab seat so that if anybody would attempt to rob me I would not have anything on me.

One Sunday morning just before day, an open call came in. I'd had a good night and I decide to take this call and then I would go in. The dispatcher told me the number of the street and told me that it was upstairs. I was to go up there and knock on the door. I knocked on the door and a lady said to come in. She needed me to help her take her luggage down. When I walked in she was in her negligee. Then she told me to shut the door. When I shut the door I froze in my tracks like an icicle in Alaska. I said to myself, "What am I into?" I thought of how Willie McGee was executed about something like this in Mississippi. I thought of all of the other men I had known who were

71

lynched because of situations like this. I said to myself, "If I don't cooperate with her she may holler 'rape.' If I cooperate with her my chances may be better for getting out of here." She ordered me to take off my clothes. I did and she took my hand and led me to the bed. After that ordeal, she told me to go in the bathroom and wash up and asked me if I was satisfied. I said, "Yes," and she said, "That will cost you fifteen dollars." I gave her the money and rushed out of there and went back to my cab. Those were some of the things that happened to me while driving a cab. Cab driving was dangerous to a great extent. I always wanted to drive a cab all of my life and to work in a hotel. Unfortunately, I never did get a chance to work in a hotel.

Shortly after that, during the wintertime, I had a couple bumpers. It wasn't my fault. It was company policy that if you had two or three bumpers like that you had to report it. It didn't hurt the cab or anything. I didn't know it at that time, but what they were really afraid of was people suing for everything. That's what they were concerned about. Therefore, I got fired from that job. I really enjoyed it while I was there.

I had gotten acquainted with another one of my classmates, Emma Alice Rodgers (she had married then but that's all that I knew her by). I got to be really good friends with her and her brother-in-law, William Stits, and his wife. She told me about how she had qualified to be a teacher up there and she tried to get me to get qualified. I wasn't too sure if I wanted to teach up there and I didn't get qualified. But eventually, my friend, S.T. Nero, had started substitute teaching up there. I was working on a real poor job, so, I started substitute teaching. I went around to a couple of schools. Then I was talking to S.T. and he was telling me about his teaching position. It so happened, that I got called to the school where he was working. He told me to talk to the principal, Mr. John Finlacy. It was a school on Douglas Boulevard. I could walk from home to the school.

And that's what I did. I ran into a couple of bad boys in Chicago; one of them when I first went to work. This boy was bad and he wouldn't sit down. He would get up and give me the laws about if I did this to him what he would do and his mother would sue me. I wasn't afraid of a lawsuit then. I worked around there and would tell him to sit down and I pleaded with him and pleaded with him. I was at the desk one day. I looked in the desk drawer and there was a belt, a pulley belt. It was a nice strap rolled in there. I got the strap out of the drawer and eased it into my pocket and he didn't see it. He kept telling me that if I hit him I would be arrested. I just kept pleading with him. I got up to him and I grabbed him by his collar. I took that belt out of my pocket and I tore that little ole boy *up*! Fortunately for me, I got out of school before he did and I went by his house. I told his mother what I had done. She said, "Mr. McCullough, I am so glad that you did that because these other teachers won't whip these children. They let them have their way and half of them don't ever learn anything."

He came back the next day and I asked him, "Did you tell your mother?"

He answered me with a snappy attitude, "No."

I said, "Why didn't you tell her?" I know he told her but what had happened she told him that I had been by and talked with her. After that I didn't have any more trouble with him.

At Theodore Herzel School I had a little problem. It was a boy there; he was in the eighth grade and he was supposed to be smart. He was making noise. He would look at me and he knew exactly when I would see him. I never could catch who it was making the noise. He kept making this noise. I decided to get in the back of the room. What I did, I walked to one corner of the room. In the corner at the back you could see every time anyone would move. So when he made a noise and looked back, I saw where it was coming. I didn't have no strap so I just walked over there where he was. When I got to him, I caught him in the collar and I lifted him up out of his seat and slapped him real hard and shoved him back down in the seat and told him, "Don't you ever make a noise in my room!" From that day on, you could hear water dropping on cotton in my room. I think the principal heard about it and he asked me to be a regular substitute teacher and I worked every day from then on. That's where I got my experience in dealing with those little bad boys in Chicago.

Six

In the meantime, my family had a family reunion in July. I came back down to Canton. I wanted to talk to Betty Smith. She told me to come by because she wanted to go to the family reunion with me. So, I went to pick her up and she was not there. I was mad about that. After the closing of our reunion that Sunday, I went back to Chicago. On the way I stopped by where she was working. I saw her and I talked to her and we got into an argument and I slapped her lightly. I did apologize. At that time I could hit a cow in the ribs and knock it down. I was not trying to hurt her. Therefore, I did apologize. I was in another county and I knew what they would do when they put people in jail. I had never been in jail so I didn't want to be in jail. Anyway, after that confrontation I left.

I went on back to Chicago. The next thing I knew, they had trumped up some charges on me. They wanted me for attempted murder! I blamed Governor Coleman for that today. Everybody talked about what a good governor he was, but to me he wasn't much to allow people to do that. He should have asked those people what did I do. I knew what I had done. It was just a misdemeanor. I know I didn't have any business slapping her, but I did. Well, they took it and made a big issue out of it. They sent up there to Chicago to have me expedited back to Mississippi. That was in the summer of 1956. They had the charges trumped up and papers made out on me. When I got off work one evening, I saw two big white men standing in our yard. I never had seen white folk in anyone's yard. I had seen a few Jews up there but no white folk. I didn't pay them any mind. Just as I passed by them they pulled a gun on me! They said I was under arrest.

I said, "Under arrest for what?"

He said, "We got a warrant for you from Mississippi."

"For what?" I said.

He said, "They want you for attempted murder."

I said, "No, you must have the wrong person."

"No, we got the papers to show you," he said.

So, they took me to jail. They put me in that little holding pen. That was the worst night I've ever had in my life! I think now I have some kind of phobia and can't stand to be in any kind of closed place. I didn't know how to feel and I didn't know what to do! I had to stay there all night on that hard bench! I wasn't used to nothing like that.

When morning came, they took me to a worst place, Cook County Jail. While I was over there I heard one of the workers say, "Where are we going to put him?"

The other one said, "Put him down there with the other bad folks."

I was wondering what they were talking about. Down there where they put me was with all the murderers. I ran into a boy down there who was in for murder. It was a white fellow in there about as tall as I was. I didn't worry about getting his name or any of my cellmates' names. I was too concerned about how I was going to get out of there. I got my mother word down in Mississippi. They sent my brother Willot and he got a lawyer, Cecil Parte. Attorney Parte came and got me out and I stayed out there. I really wanted to come back and go to Caroll County and turn myself in. But Mother told me not to.

What she was thinking about was all they had written up about me and what they were going to do. She figured that the folk in Caroll County were going to send me to prison. So, I didn't go.

The time came when I was supposed to go back to court. They put me back in jail and waited for the sheriff of Caroll County to come up there. He brought me back to Mississippi. It was a white fellow up there that they wanted, also. So, they put us both in the car with our hands cuffed behind us. We got to talking with him. He saw we were not trying to escape or nothing so he really started to loosen up and began to talk with us. I was afraid because I figured they were going to send me to Parchman. I couldn't pick any cotton so, I knew I was going to be in for a hard time! I got to talking to him and we asked him to take the handcuffs off of one our hands and handcuff us together. He agreed to do it. That made it a little more comfortable to ride from way up there. When we got to talking, I asked him how could I get out of it. He said, "If you give me a thousand dollars you won't go nowhere." Of course, I was tempted to give it to him because I had offered the girl two thousand to drop the charges. They wouldn't let her do it; I know that's what it was.

So, we wound up down there in Vaiden. I came in and my mother and my brother, Willot, met me when we got there to the county jail in Vaiden. They came up there and got me. I came on to Canton and got a lawyer, Mrs. Hood. Now, Mrs. Hood wanted to know the facts. She said, "Now, you tell me the truth! It is a lot of innocent people in jail, but you tell me the truth. I wouldn't want you to be in jail if you are innocent." I told her the truth. She said, "You give me a hundred and twenty-five dollars and I will meet you in court. Then you'll need to give me another hundred and twenty-five dollars so that I can hire a lawyer to work with me in that county." So, I gave her two hundred and fifty dollars. She took the case.

While we were waiting for the case to come up on the court docket, I was in the park over on Davis Crossing and Highway 51, a nice pine park. I was sitting in my car playing the radio. A highway patrolman came in there and got out of his car. I wandered what he wanted because I wasn't doing anything. He came over there, pulled his pistol out and said, "Nigger, what you doing in this park. You either get out of this goddamned park or I'll blow your damn brains out!" Here I am worrying about this other court deal and then here comes a highway patrolman talking like that. I didn't say one word. I cranked the car up and left because I knew that if I had any kind of conflict with him I would have been in prison for life for absolutely nothing. Therefore, I escaped that.

The day came for me to go to court. Mrs. Hood and my other lawyer were there. Judge Miles was presiding over my case. He was telling it to the court how the time had changed and it would not be like it used to be. Now, this was right in the heat of the civil rights movement. With his position in government, he could see how things were going to change. He said that things never would be the same. After we went through court, it was obvious that they had mistreated me so bad and nothing I could do about it. They had the trial and they decided that they would not give me any time. They gave me probation and a fine. It cost me five hundred dollars for the court cost and expenses to bring me back to Mississippi. Since I had a job, they told me that I could go on back to Chicago to my job. That's what I did. The sheriff was named David Bennett. I didn't blame the sheriff as much as I blamed the governor for signing the papers when he knew that I had done nothing.

When my court case was over, I went back to Chicago to Parte's office. I asked him to give me my money back. He was really surprised to see me because he thought I was not going to get out jail. Then I went back to work. I changed jobs. I had been working a little for a ladies apparel shop. They only sold ladies shoes down on Halster Street. I went over to Barnes Air King after seeing the advertisement in the paper. While working there I ran into a fellow, named Latin V. Major. We got to know each other pretty good. I would pick him up every morning. He liked to discuss history and at that time the Soviet Union was strong.

A magazine about the Soviet Union was being printed and distributed here in the U.S. and the U.S. was printing and distributing a magazine about America over there. I used to listen to the news and they were talking about how pitiful people were over there. He and I were discussing this issue. I would talk about what I had heard on television and radio. He would discuss what he had read in the magazine. So, he persuaded me to start taking the magazine. I started reading the magazine and I saw all of the things that they said about the Soviet Union were not true. It was all propaganda. In one issue of the magazine they had a tour going to Russia. I decided to go. I called down there and made reservations and they told me that it would cost me fifteen hundred dollars to go and stay fifteen days. That's what I did.

Seven

The fifteen-day tour was to take place in June. I wasn't going to Moscow in bad weather months. So, I went from Chicago to Montreal in Canada. We fueled up there. The next stop we made was in London and I spent the night there in a hotel. I decided to get out and look at some of the pubs that they are renowned for. England was pretty much the same as America. Yet, I didn't go too far. I didn't try to look for anything. I just looked at those pubs they had. I went back to my hotel and stayed there until it was time to go. We left there. One thing I can say, at that time, the British had the best pilots in the air. They could set a plane down and you wouldn't know when you hit the ground. I had a chance to see that twice. I went over there on TWA. That airline was popular at that time. I was real impressed with the pilots' skills.

When I left there I got on a Russian plane. Those pilots were not nearly as good as the British pilots. When they would touch down they would bounce three or four times, pretty rough. I don't like to fly with a pilot that bounces around but I made it there. In June, it was nice when I got over there. The grass was all green. It looked good at that time. We went into the hotel and I got my room assignment and checked in. I decided to come back out and just really have a look around at the people since I had been told how pitiful they were and how sorry they looked.

When I got out there, I could not see any difference in them than in any other people. I carried a bag of chewing gum and passed it out to all of the children on the street. Every child I saw I had to give them gum and show them how to chew it. Every child in Moscow was looking for me from that point on. So, standing around in the hotel, and of course the people that went over there with me . . . they wanted to stay as far away from me as they possibly could. Just like they were doing over here in America. We had segregation. I got there and they were saying they were going up to the American Embassy. I said to myself, "I didn't come way over here to see no Americans. I saw enough of them at home."

So, I decided since I heard them talking about Russia having good movies (and they did, they were showing resources and how they were harvested), and it was really a family picture not like ours where you can't bring your children. I decided to go to the movie. I went out there and they had a pretty long line. There were about forty or so in front of me. I could see the ticket agent and he quit selling tickets. He came out there and he beckoned for me to follow him. So I followed him. I didn't get a ticket. So he took me on in there and showed me one of the best seats in the theater and that's where I stayed and watched the picture until it was over and then I went back to the hotel.

The next morning I got up early and I went walking. I couldn't speak their language. I discovered then how good the Russian Education System really was. I was able to see how it was working, because the first thing I saw that morning was some little children. They were about five or six years old and looked like they were beginners in school and those children were walking just like soldiers down the road and nobody acting up. They were so well disciplined. I observed that. Then, I saw a train coming. I said, "I believe I will go down to the depot."

In the meantime, I was out there on the street. I did not see a piece of paper. I did not see anything on the ground. The streets were just as clean as your house. Soon as I got to the depot and it was even cleaner. The floor was shiny and they had some kind of marble floors. While I was in there I started speaking to people, I couldn't speak their language, but they could talk to me. They were speaking to me and shaking hands with me. I tell you the truth, I was in there a few minutes and that depot was full. Those folks surrounded me, trying to shake hands and speak to me and the police had to come in and get me out.

So, when I got out, I had missed the first place that we were supposed to visit. That was Stalin and Lenin's tomb, and I missed it. I didn't see that. In the meantime, when we got on the bus, I was used to riding on the back of the bus, and I did not like to ride on the back of the bus. . . . I liked to ride on the front seat. Consequently, the guide would sit with me. Another thing I learned about the Russian educational system at that time: If you meet ten people out there, one of them could speak French, one could speak English and the other could speak Spanish. I had never seen anything like it, but that's the way it was over there.

So, when we went on the next tour, they were all getting away from me back in the back of the bus. So, we got to a park and that park had Lenin's picture growing in the grass and it looked just as real as it does in a book. I had never seen anything like it. And I went out there and there was an old man standing out there by himself. He had the longest beard I had ever seen on a man. And I walked up to him since all of the other folks were going the other way and I was by myself. So, I walked up to him and shook hands with him. This old man could not speak my language and I couldn't speak his. We smiled at each other. So, I just reached down and got his beard and tied it around my neck! And of course he really smiled! Then all of the Russians out there in that park came to greet me. The other people on the tour with me never did know what happened and I never did tell them what happened. And everybody came to shake hands with me.

The people in Russia were not paying the rest of the tourists any attention. So, on our way back to the hotel, there was a lady from Canada. She said, "If you want to be noticed, you better be with Jessie, because it looks like they'll just about run over you to get to him." Then they started trying to sit with me. And I was really popular then. So, the time we spent in Moscow, I believe, was about five days. I guess I was the most popular man in Moscow at that time.

When we left, I think we went to Kiev. Now they want to sit with me. They decided they were not going to isolate me any more. So, we went to Kiev and we did not stay there too long, maybe about two or three days. The tour was only for fifteen days and we visited about three or four cities. We left there and went to Leningrad, now it is called it Petrograd. I had a chance to visit all of the czar's wealth and possessions that he owned. Then they would give us the history. And it was a really interesting tour because it was Leningrad that the Germans seized, Leningrad and Moscow. They were telling me about the siege and how people were starving and some of the folks would steal one another's babies and kill the baby and eat the baby. And that is a type of thing that we never heard of. But they told me about that over there. I really felt kind of sorry for them. After the war was over they had kind of got themselves together. I can understand why our folks were talking about how pitiful they looked during wartime and they were surrounded by the Germans. I guess everybody would have been because the German soldiers were really tough on people.

After we left Leningrad, we went to Yalta. That's where we spent the most of our time. I used to get up early in the morning as I did that morning. So, when I got up and I saw people going swimming in the Black Sea. That's where Churchill, Roosevelt, and Stalin had sat on that bench and had their picture made the "Big 3." I had a chance to sit on that bench and we entertained on the bench. I made a lot of friends there. These people would go way out in the sea early in the morning and I wondered how in the world they would stay out there so long. It would probably be twelve o'clock before they would come back out of the water. I decided that I was going to get up and try it.

The next morning I put on my swimming suit and I went out there. I started out and got about thirty or forty yards out in the sea and I caught a cramp. I had taken cramps in the water before, so I wasn't really surprised. So I just flipped on my back and floated on back to the bank. While I was out lying around in the sand, I noticed everybody was coming by looking at me. You know, I was thinking what would happen if I was out by myself and out on the beach like that back home. I was kind of suspicious. There was a lady that had the nerve enough to come up to me and ask me, "Let me feel your hair." Well, we've always been taught our hair was ugly and nappy. Of course, I never did adhere to that. I always felt that we have curly hair. Those of us who don't have curly hair have wavy hair. Those who have wavy hair was mixed with Caucasian and black and that's why they had wavy hair. Once one of them came up to me then everybody over there wanted to feel my hair and talked about how pretty it was. That gave me an opportunity to compare cultures. The culture over there did not degrade our hair. I met a major in the army there and his wife and she was a doctor. Of course, that's where I really learned about the salaries. We got into a discussion about the salaries of people and everything and about what you can rent an apartment. A single apartment would rent for $6.00 a month (well it translated to about $6.00 a month) and the double apartment rented for about $12.00. That's why I was concerned about how much salary was being made and she told me the doctors over there make $150.00 a month and of course that was amazing to me. I know our doctors probably charge you that in a day.

But anyway, they started wining and dining me. They wanted me to stay around them and we began discussing the system. He was telling me that the Soviet Union was the strongest power on earth and everything like that. So, I brought up the parties. He asked me in his language, "ye comonis?" Finally I understood what he had said. He asked me was I a Communist. I said, "No, I'm a Democrat." Of course, he didn't know what a Democrat was. Then I had to kind of explain to him that we had a two-party system—Democrat and Republican. We just got along so well until they wanted me to be with them all of the time and I spent all my time with them. They would take me to lunch every day. I just had the biggest time and in the evening time when they would go in, I would meet the girls. And, oh man, they would ask to feel my hair and play with my hair and rub my skin. Apparently some of those people had never seen black folks. I know they were supposed to have one slave (I found that out from the major), they did have one slave in Moscow back during the era of slavery and his name was Pushkin and they had a street in Moscow named Pushkin. They were talking about how smart he was and he got to be in the King's court. You know everybody didn't go to Moscow at that time. So, they just had not seen many black people. Well, I stayed there and we had a good time all the while I was there. In fact, that was the best vacation and the only vacation I ever had until 1999 when my family and I went to Florida. Up until that time I had never been on a vacation that I enjoyed so much.

Then the time came for me to come back. I came back to Moscow. I really enjoyed that. I found out they were not as unhappy as a lot of folks had said they were. The news media had misinformed us altogether. Those people were just as happy as a lark at that time. I don't know how they are now since they have gotten away from that system, but they sure were happy when I was over there. After I landed in Moscow and we went and got our baggage ready and they took us back to the airport. They flew us back to London and there we boarded the plane in London and had a good pilot from London. They flew us back into Montreal. Then I had to catch one of those other planes; it wasn't a jet. That was the roughest ride I had ever had and I could see the sparks from that engine and I really didn't enjoy that flight at all from Montreal back to Chicago. I was so glad when I got back to Chicago I didn't know what to do.

While working in Chicago, I had decided that the integration was getting hotter and hotter. My daddy had asked me to come and take over his farm for him. Of course, I could see what he was talking about. He had gotten too old to see about it and right now I'm reaching that age where I feel the same way. So, I decided to come on back. I felt like if I didn't get into the school system before they integrated, then blacks, as teachers were not going to be able to get into the school system.

So, that's why I came back before they integrated completely. I got back here and my friend had talked to me about a job. James Goodloe, he was principal at Velma Jackson in Camden, Mississippi. I also ran into another friend of mine who was a schoolmate, James Jones, Jr. He was the principal at Rogers High in Canton, Mississippi. So, I took the job with Principal Jones.

My Life during the Change in Mississippi

Rev. Clifton Goodloe, Sr. had started preaching and had gotten to be a bishop. He had heard I was going into the cattle business. I wanted to get my pasture land fixed up to put the cows in it. He had some cows and he wanted me to come over and look at them. He wanted to sell his cattle because he was going to be too busy with his church work. He wasn't going to have time for his cows. He also told me that he would rent his pasture to me. So, I decided to take him up on that. I was working on my fences and we had a few cows in there. I had started buying cows.

After we fixed up my pastor and everything, I brought the cows home. I later found some more in the newspaper. Mr. Mackey started me to taking that paper and I take that paper now. It is the *Mississippi Bulletin*. That's where I found those cows, way up in Webster County. I brought them home and put them in the pasture along with my other cattle, which was a mistake. A couple of those cows that I had bought from Webster County were infected with what we call "bang disease." It spread through my herd! I had a hard time getting that herd clean. However, eventually I did get it clean. I was trying to get my herd up to a hundred head.

Now, back to the schools. I finally took the job with Principal Jones. I was trying to figure out what I was going to do. I hadn't yet made up my mind on how I was going to handle it. After getting the school job, one day I was in Jackson riding around and I saw a service station it was a Sinclare Station. It looked new and clean. I had always wanted a service station. I had wanted one while I was in Chicago but I was never able to get it. I decided to go by this one and look at it. It had a sign out front for rent. So, I got the number off it and called the agent.

Finally, I was able to catch up with him and one day I met him over there. He showed me the property. He was impressed with me wanting to manage the service station. I told him I wanted to get it and let my brother Clarence run it for me. He said, "Well, if you were getting this for yourself, I wouldn't hesitate to let you have it, this is your money. But if you invest five thousand dollars in a business and you are going to have somebody else run it, I wouldn't recommend that at all." But I talked with him and finally I convinced him to let us try it. He did but he told me, "This type of operation has failed so many times. I hate to see you put your money into it. But since you are so willing and you think you can handle it, I will let you have it. When you get the station, one thing you need to do. You see how clean it looks right now? Keep your restrooms clean and keep the front of your station clean. Just keep everything clean around it." At that time he said, "You know, whites don't hardly trade with blacks, but if you will keep this station clean they won't know whether you are black or white."

So, I did. He let me have it and we got it stocked up. That summer we were finally able to get the station opened. I stayed there and I was the manager then until school started. I had a contract with the Canton Separate School District. I was trying to get the station running before school opened. And I did. I ran it across the summer and we did really well. I left it stocked up really good. We had right at two thousand dollars in the bank. I thought we would be off and running good and we wouldn't have any more trouble.

My brother, Tommy Lee, and I were talking. He was really familiar with the single women in Jackson. I had told him that I felt it was time for me to settle down. He asked me what type of lady did I want to meet, whether I wanted to meet a young woman or an older lady. At that time, I had just about made up my mind that I did not want to become affiliated with a younger woman because I saw the problems older men had marrying younger women. Of course I tried my best to guide my life by other people's mistakes. Sometimes you do that and you still don't come out right, but it did work out.

At that time, I wasn't used to seeing black people with credit cards. A couple of nice looking young ladies came by there and they paid for their gas on credit cards. I didn't try to make contact with them because I figured they were not in my class. Tommy Lee introduced me to another lady. Of course, she had been married and she had two children and I said, "Well, it is a possibility that since this lady has children we would be able to raise our own family. It was possible that we could continue to have a nice little family." I wanted to have one or two children and that would be fine. It didn't work out that way, but I got together with this lady at that time. She had really long, pretty hair. That's the woman I married, named Kattie. So, things were going well. My main thing was that I was always crazy about women with long hair and right now I don't think anything on earth is any prettier than a woman with a beautiful head of hair.

My brother Clarence whom we called Bear ran the station through the fall. But just as the agent had told me, it came out that way. Around January of the next year, we didn't have money to restock with. What really happened, my brother would leave other people there and he would go around to see about civil rights with Medgar Evers. He was the kind of manager that would leave other people there and they would put money in their pockets.

That January I had to borrow money to restock it with and to keep us going. We kept it there until school was out and then I got all of my pasture work finished up and then I went down there to help him to run it. He decided he wanted to go to Kansas City to visit his nieces and nephews. He did. He left and I ran it until he came back, but I stayed until school was ready to open. When he came back, I had the station restocked and had about sixteen hundred dollars in the bank. I figured this time that maybe he would make a run of it.

In the meantime I began having trouble with law enforcers. At that time Interstate 55 ended up at Canton. You could get on it and never run into any officers. The lights didn't work on an old truck that I drove. They would cut on and off at night. When I would get on 55 I could cut them off until I got to Tougaloo. I would put my lights on when I got on County Line Road. Then I would get on Bailey Avenue and drive on in to where I lived on Albemarle Road. Wasn't much traffic on any of those roads at that time. I never did run into a police at night on those roads when I was traveling.

During that time, the officers were on the highways and in the cities stopping black people and giving tickets.

I was coming from a ballgame one night, coming out of Adeline St. to what is now called Martin Luther King Drive. I had been coming out there all the time. So, I came in from a ballgame and the police were waiting on me, I suppose. So they gave me a ticket there and said I ran the stop sign. So, the next morning on my way to work at the school I raced back over to see whether or not there was a stop sign. I said, "Ain't no stop sign there."

I went to the police station and Mr. Dan Thomas was the chief of police at that time. I carried the ticket to him and said, "Mr. Thomas, the officer stopped me last night and gave me a ticket and said I ran a stop sign. I wish you would have an officer to go back over there and see that there isn't a stop sign there."

He said, "Give me your ticket."

I gave him my ticket and he called the officer and had him to go back to see if there was a stop sign there or not. So, he went and when he came back he was dragging around the place a while. Mr. Thomas said, "Well, was there a stop sign there."

He said, "No, sir, but there was supposed to be."

Mr. Thomas said, "Well, you don't give people tickets on 'supposes'."

This is what happened after getting that ticket on Adeline and Martin Luther King Drive. I came up with a scheme and it worked pretty well. When I'm on the highway, usually I try to drive into the city behind a white person. For a long time I didn't have any trouble. I would always write the tag number down of the person I was behind. Somehow or another I was going into Canton one morning I was coming in on Highway 16.

I got behind a white lady and my mind told me to take her tag number and I took the number down. We got to the Number 2 Fire Station (it wasn't there at that time) and so they pulled her over and checked her driver's license and waved her on. So, then they pulled me over and beckoned for me to come on up to them. I had my driver's license and I was ready to pass them out and I did. I figured they were going to do me the same way. But it didn't work out that way. I handed them my driver's license and he said, "Nigger, what you doing speeding up and down this road?" And that kind of stunned me.

I said, "Officer, how could I be speeding and I was driving behind this lady that you just let go and she wasn't speeding."

He said, "You one of them smart son of a bitches. I'll put your black ass in jail." Of course, I didn't say anything. So, I took that ticket.

So I took that ticket in to the chief of police and I said, "Well, Mr. Thomas, I have another ticket here. The officer stopped me and said I was speeding. But I was traveling behind another lady and I wrote her tag number down. This is the lady's tag number that I was following. They pulled her over and checked her license and waved her on. Then, they pulled me over and said I was speeding and gave me a ticket and a terrible verbal abuse." So he took that ticket and he tore it up. That was the second ticket I had gotten. So that lasted a while.

I didn't have any more trouble with the police until later on I was clipping my pasture beside a road known now as the Riley Williams Road. My pasture was looking good and prospering with white clovers and everything. I had done what the county agent had told me to and I really had a good pasture that was just as green as it could be. I noticed Sheriff Billy Noble came in and went on back in there to a gentleman's house by the name of Tom Grant. So, when he came out I was trying to get through clipping. At that time I was living in Jackson. And he beckoned for me to come to the fence. I got off the tractor and I said to myself, "I wonder what this man want with me?

"I have a warrant for you," he told me.

I said, "For what?"

He said, "For murder."

I said, "Who did I kill and where did I kill him?"

"In Chicago," he said. "I'm not gonna take you in now. You just stay where I can put my hands on you." So he left and he really had me upset. I was very concerned about this because I knew it was possible for people to have the same name and get mixed up.

That's why when I finished that night I went on back to Jackson. Sunday morning I got up early and I called the Eleventh Street Station in Chicago and I asked them if they had a warrant out for me. The man asked me my name and I told him my name and he said, "Well, I'll look it up." So he looked it up and said, "No, I don't have no warrant for anybody by that name." So, then I felt good and I said, "Now, the sheriff has lied." I said, "I wonder why he told that lie." I didn't say anything to him and he never did say anything to me. So, I didn't have any more conflicts with the sheriff then until Martin Luther King came to Canton that night.

I had come to Canton to participate in that march. We pitched a tent over there where Nichols Middle School is now; it was not there at that time. Of course, that's the night they shot the tear gas on us. I had never been involved in tear gas before. That was about one of the worst things I ever had contact with! They threw this tear gas at us that looked like hand grenades. They filled the tent up with that stuff.

So after that, I got around to trying to run my business. My brother Tommy Lee and my brother, W.E.L. (we called him Mule), his name was so long we just used his initials, they had told me that I had better be ready to take over the station in two years because Bear wasn't going to stay there no longer than two years. Sure enough, he ran it down and I had to take it over. The stock was low and I decided to sell. I sold it to another gentleman. I lost about four thousand dollars on that operation. Then I was able to put all of my time in the farm up here along with the job I had at school.

So one day, I was in town and I walked the street and I ran into Billy Noble. Somehow or another he and I got into it again. The sheriff started walking towards me and he said, "I'll blow your damn brains out." When he made that step and said what he said then I stepped up close to him so if he decided to go for his gun, at least I would have an opportunity to take it. He said, "Well, that's not gonna solve the problem." And I said, "No, that won't solve it." So, then I left.

*　　*　　*

So at this time, I learned to plant rye grass for the cattle. So I had about thirty-three acres I wanted to plant rye grass on. I really had more than that, but I didn't have the tractor to break it up. So, I talked with my cousin, Otha Williams, and we called him Buddy Fronie. He told me to come up there and get his tractor. I went and got his tractor. It was so much faster and I got the work done so quickly that I decided then that I needed a heavier tractor. So, I went down to Smith Tractors. Smith Tractors had a little tractor that was nice, but it still wasn't as heavy as it should have been. But I didn't know about weight at that time. So, I bought it and finally I saw that it wasn't going to do. I was down in Jackson for some reason and I ran across a dealer out there on Highway 80. There was a place out there selling tractors and there was a Massey Ferguson Tractor. So, I stopped in there and he had a 1080. He recommended it to me and of course I traded my Ford for it. I got that tractor and it was really just what I needed to break up the land. At that time, the tractor could carry a twelve-foot disk. I finally found a disk to put to the tractor.

I found that disk in the *Mississippi Bulletin* paper. I went up there and got it in West Point. It was the ideal thing. I could get my work done in a day when before it had taken a week to complete. That's when I really learned to do that. But, in the meantime, while I was doing that I would get through planting so quickly that I wouldn't have anything for the tractor to do. So, I remember I went over and I broke up a field for my cousin. I disked his field for him and turned all of that grass under. That way I was helping more and more people. That was just to have something to do. I didn't even charge him. Fuel was about $0.18 gallon. It was not much more, I know. Anyway, I had the tractor and nothing to do, so I would attend civil rights meetings for a little while.

Finally, some of the white citizens got concerned about me. It wasn't anything I was doing, but I would probably go to a meeting once a week. One of my friends, James Goodloe (we talked about every day), he asked me, "What are you doing?"

I said, "Like what?"

He said, "Man, these white folks sure are talking about getting rid of you." So, that went on for a while. At that time, Mr. Allen was superintendent. And I had worked everything out and everything started looking good. So, I figured if they did stop me from teaching school, I wouldn't have the money then to carry on my farm operation.

At that time, I had bought some hay equipment to cut my own hay and everything just began to fall in place. I worked like that a while and they had been trying to get Mr. Allen to fire me. I learned that and he wouldn't do it. I worked under those conditions until the middle of the '65 and '66 school term. At the closing of that term (you would get your contract early in the year), Principal Jones told me they were not going to re-hire me. Well, what had happened is that year they had brought in a new superintendent. Mr. Allen was replaced by Lamar Fortenberry. So, Lamar Fortenberry was brought in to fire me and that's what he did.

So, I went back to talk with the board about it. I got an appointment with the board. I was able to get a meeting with the school board on the 24th of May and asked them to reconsider. Of course, I saw something that night when the board met. When I saw Charlie Riddell come in I knew I was not going to get a new contract. The members of the board at that time were Grady Morgan, Charlie Riddell, Dr. Flynn, Tommie James and Rudy Holmes. Some of the members were late arriving to the meeting. They were trying to wait for Dr. Flynn to come to the meeting. However, Dr. Flynn knew it was wrong for them to fire me, therefore, he did not show up. They were just trying to get him in on their scheme, but he wouldn't take part in it.

Of course, I learned later on that this is what they said. "In reference to your meeting, the Canton Municipal Separate School District Board on May 24, 1966, we considered your case very carefully, but decided that it could not offer you employment because you have not been recommended to the board as required by section 6T8T-07 of

the Mississippi Code. Sincerely, Lamar Fortenberry. . . ."
Of course, that terminated my employment with the Canton Municipal Separate School District.

The white folks were trying to run me out of Madison County. They told Mr. James Jones, Jr. to tell me if I wanted to teach school to go to another county. After the way they treated me, I told Mr. Jones to tell them wasn't no s.o.b. going to tell me where to go.

About that time they had started hiring blacks in government agencies such as FHA and ASC, so I applied at the ASC Service. I got hired to measure land in Madison County. Clifton Goodloe, Jr. came back home about that time to take over his father's farming operation. I told him about the hiring at these agencies and I carried him to the ASC Service and he got hired, too. However, he had a longer term with them than I did. I worked there for three months and then they terminated me.

I had met a fellow, Rutherford Rousier, while I was running my service station. After I was terminated from the ASC he gave me a part time job at Security Life Insurance Co. I made about forty dollars a week. I worked there for about two years. Then I began to work for a government program called the STAR program. I was assigned to Durant. I was teaching people how to apply for jobs and teaching them simple math and assisted them in finding jobs in the factories at that time. That's where I met a man named Kilibrew. He was an alderman in Durant and he was very helpful to me while we were running that program. He was also a salesman at Hands Motor Company. He sold me my first Ford truck. I had printed on the side of that truck, "I Shall Return." The white folk were concerned about what the message meant. I told them that it meant just what it said. They were thinking that I was going to return to teaching school.

During that time Clifton worked at the ACS he was also farming. I had this tractor and it wasn't doing anything and the fuel was really cheap. So, I used to take the tractor and help him with his crop.

Eventually, I decided to start row cropping myself. Clifton had bought a combine and I was able to get him to harvest for me and I planted forty acres of beans. That was the beginning of me going into row cropping. Next year I was able to get thirty more acres from Charlie James. He had decided that he was not going to farm any more. He had gotten a job down at Madison Wood Works. So, he rented me his thirty acres and that increased my acreage. We started like that and I worked with Clifton and helped him to plant. I told him, "Cliff, since you are depending on this for your living we will go ahead and finish yours first because I don't have that much." That's the way we operated.

Time passed. My cousin, Otha Williams, we called him Buddy Fronie, he was indebted to the FHA. They were going to foreclose on him. He had seventy acres of land that he wanted to sell. He sent me word that he wanted to sell it and asked if I wanted to buy it. So, I decided that I would try to buy it from him. I went to the Federal Land Bank to see if they would finance it. They told me that they would finance it. I showed them the land that I had which was forty acres in the swamp. The loan officer agreed to make the loan to me under those conditions. When I went back to try to follow through on the loan, he told me that he would not make me a loan on that land. So, just happened that I had the map with me of my daddy's land that adjoined my swamp land. I said, "If I had this would you make me a loan?" He said, "Oh, yes." He was thinking that I couldn't get that. He didn't know that it belonged to my father; I didn't tell him.

So, I left his office and I came back home and told my daddy what I needed to do and my daddy agreed. We went right on and exchanged; I traded him my forty for his forty acres so that I could get the loan to buy the land from my cousin. When I went back, the loan officer was surprised and he still fooled around because I understand that some white folk up here had told him that they wanted to buy that land. They didn't want him to finance it for me. If I couldn't get it financed then, of course, the white people would be able to buy it. At that time I decided that I was going through with it. I drove down to the headquarters in New Orleans. I went there and told them what had happened. They went to work and made me the loan. That's how I got the farm loan.

Eight

The land was real good land because he had just cleaned up a new ground back there and I didn't know that because he had one of those bulldozers to cut the stumps off even with the ground and you wouldn't know it. So, when I went down there to break up the land, I couldn't tell it was new ground. When I got through breaking it (we planted it flat), I went in there with my cultivator. I was breaking everything on the cultivator every time I moved. I was always tearing up something. So, I had to come out of there with the tractor and get me some mules. I had Albert Sims to come over there and help me to get the land worked out. We made a beautiful crop on it! However, that July high water came and drowned that entire crop out back there. That left me in debt.

As farmers do, we have to expand to try to make up for the loss when something happens like that. That year I needed to expand and my brother-in-law, Levy Westbrook, he married my half-sister, Leora, he had gotten sick and wasn't able to work his land. He let me have his. In the meantime, Preston Winfield's children had grown up and he was indebted to the FHA. Buddy Mansel was trying to get the FHA to foreclose on him so that the could get the land. Just so happened, I ran into him and he told me that he would rent it to me. I told him, "Well, we have to go down to the FHA office and have them to agree on it."

100

When I went there, the first officer I met with wouldn't let me have it. He said, "No, he can't rent land." That was a policy of FHA. So, he turned me down. I didn't know it, but Joe Dockins, a black fellow working there told me that one of the higher officers from Jackson told them, "Gentlemen, you all know that is wrong. If that man can rent his land and pay his notes, you ought to let him do it." That changed their minds and possibly the agency policy, too, because they decided that they would let me rent it. Somehow, Joe got me word and I went down there. What I had to do was to pay two notes to catch up and that way I was allowed to work that land.

After expanding like I did, I needed a heavier tractor. I went down to the John Deere place in Canton to talk with them about buying a 4020. So happened, I met a farmer who was familiar with tractors, Charles Hoggins. He told me, "McCullough, you need to get a heavier tractor for the land you have. Get you a 4320. That will be big enough to handle whatever you are going to do on your farm." So, I went back down to the John Deere place in Canton to talk with them about a 4320. They wouldn't even talk with me. But for some reason, Massey Ferguson had put a dealership in Yazoo City. Somehow, a fellow over there named John Warren, a salesman, had heard about me needing a heavier tractor. He came over here and I was in the field. I was driving a 1080. When I bought it I didn't get a manual so I didn't understand how to operate it. So he came out there and showed me all of those things. That impressed me. Then he wanted to sell me a heavier tractor. I agreed to do it. I wound up buying an 1150. That one had a hundred-horse power and that was all I needed to do my work in the fields.

Before, I had been able to let Clifton Goodloe use my other tractor, but now I had to pay for this tractor. Clifton had used my other tractor to break up eighty acres on John Powell's place. Edward Sims drove it for him. He wanted to borrow this tractor like he had done before but I couldn't afford to do that. I had bought a new tractor and he had a combine and I had to pay to use his combine. He didn't want to pay to use my new tractor. That couldn't work. Anyway, we finally worked things out. Then he bought a tractor. James Goodloe bought a 4320. We somehow got to working through and through and each one of us broke up our own land. We worked together and planted. By us having three tractors, one tractor would go ahead disking and the other tractor would be harrowing because we planted flat and the last tractor would come behind and plant it. That way we always planted in the moisture. We did that for two years.

Of course, for some reason, Cliff decided that since I didn't let him use my tractor for free that he was not going to work with me anymore. He went to my cousin, Otha Williams, and encouraged him to join him and James Goodloe. It was getting close to farming time and I had expanded on this land and I was dependent on him to plant it. James Goodloe asked me, "McCullough, how are you going to plant your land this year?"

"Cliff," I said.

He said, "No, Cliff is not going to plant for you."

I said, "What?"

"No. You had better check," he said.

So, I checked around and I found out that he wasn't going to plant for me. He had made a deal with my cousin. They weren't even going to tell me about. He was going to replace me with Otha. I saw them out there in the field together but I didn't know what was going on. Just so happened, I had talked with James Goodloe and he told me that I had to plant my own crop. So, I had to buy my own planters and go to work from there.

Then I had to buy a combine and I didn't know anything about combines. I got a used combine and it gave me a lot of trouble. I had to hire somebody to help me gather that year.

I began to go to the farm sales and I learned more about combines and I was able to find a good one in Indianola. That dealer traded with me up there and I had a good combine. Really what happened, I had cut my beans up there in Camden. My combine was up there on the Winfield place. It was raining and I went up there and changed the oil in it. I didn't have a filter with me. So, when I went back up there to get my combine, I carried a filter and stuck it on there and just got on the combine and came on out with it. I brought it on down the road to finish my crop on my home place. I got up there on a hill near Mary Magdalene Cemetery and the motor cut off. I found out that all of the oil had drained out from around that filter because I had let the gasket slip. I had not put the filter on correctly. I had to send it to the shop and, of course, that combine had started to deteriorating and never work right any more. After I got it out of the shop, that combine caught afire in the field.

Then I had to buy another combine, an 850. It was one of those big combines. Since we had such trouble with cuckaburs, this one was supposed to have been improved. They said cuckaburs would not stop it. I got that one and, of course, the clutch on the throat of it was out of adjustment and it never did work right. For that reason, when the note was due that fall, I was not able to make my payment of ten thousand dollars. That spring I went to borrow the ten thousand dollars from the FHA to pay that back note. They said, "No. The only way that we will make you a note, you will have to borrow all of your farm operating money from us and give us the mortgage on your property." They forced me into getting an operating loan from FHA and from then on I was never able to get a loan from FHA. Farming went bad and I was never able to pay my notes again. The day that I closed that loan, I was unable to sleep that night.

I kept that combine a year before we got it to working right. But anyway, I was able to gather my crop. What really disappointed me was how I had helped Cliff to get established and then he would break away from me like that. I was so disappointed. I just didn't think a man would do that, yet, that happened. I got over that and from then on I was independent. Those were the kind of things that happened to me and they were a kind of a setback, too. I got to the place where I could handle my own business.

I had increased my acreage to four hundred acres. Then it was a white fellow, Atwood, he ran the Chevrolet place in Vicksburg, he had bought the Cager Sullivan Place. He had a thousand acres over there. He let me work that land. I was thinking that now since I had increased this much I would be able to pay off all of my debt. But of course, that year the price of beans was down. That year they went down and I was not able to pay my notes. I gathered twenty-four thousand bushels of beans that year and still I was in debt.

When I bought that combine, I had to have some good trucks. I bought two trucks, a Dodge truck from a contractor in Jackson and I bought a Ford from the Ford place in Canton. Eventually, I put a big bed on the Ford truck; that bed would hold five hundred bushels. So then I was able to haul my beans to Vicksburg rather than Canton. I was able to make $0.50 a bushel by carrying them to

Yazoo City and I could make a little more if I carried them to Vicksburg.

The beans were getting ripe and just about ready for me to start gathering them in the fall. I had decided to take a load on my little truck down to the co-op in Canton and sell them there to get enough money to get the tag and tires and service for both of the trucks so I could go to Vicksburg or Yazoo City or wherever I wanted to go.

The Dodge was too small to haul beans where I needed to haul. The price differences in Canton was of such nature that it would pay me to get a larger truck and haul to Yazoo or Vicksburg. The first year I decided to haul them to Vicksburg I had Dalton Swaggart driving for me. He had just retired as a truck driver and he drove them to Vicksburg. That helped me out. When we began to harvest in 1981, I decided to just take the smaller truck that would hold about three hundred bushels. Take a load down to the co-op and sell those beans there and take that money and get the tags and service on both of the trucks. On my way to the co-op, one of the highway patrolmen stopped me. I believe it was Buster Davis. When he stopped me he checked my driver's license and he called in and they said that my driver's license was out-dated. So, he immediately told me to pull the truck over and took me to jail.

Well, I had gotten a ticket down in Madison. Judge Shanks was the judge that I took the ticket to and paid for it. Well I paid the ticket with a check. The check had cleared the bank and I kept the check. When he took me to jail he knew I was a farmer. Had I been a white man, he never would have stopped me. But at that time, they were all doing everything they could to drive me out of the county. Since it was raining, he figured I would lose this load of beans. He took me on out and made me leave the beans out in the rain. Then he took me to jail. At that time Jack Pentecost was the jailor and Jack and I had established a little relation because what had happened. I needed a truck to haul some cattle to the market and Jack said yes he would do it. I paid him. Anyway that kind of built a little relationship with Jack. Jack didn't want to lock me up and he knew it wasn't necessary to lock me up because a farmer with the responsibility I had out there was no danger of me leaving on no little ticket like that.

So, Jack hesitated a long time and Buster insisted that he lock me up. So he went down there and he got one of the trustees to find a cell and they put me up there. While I was there they gave me the call and I called my wife and told her where to look and get the canceled check. She brought that down there and showed them that I had paid it. Then they let me out. In the meantime, while he was thinking the load of beans was going to be ruined, the moisture in the beans when you sell them, they always like for it to be up around thirteen percent. If it was over thirteen percent they would dock you and if it was under thirteen percent you would lose the weight. So what happened in this case, the moisture from the rain had put the moisture back up. When I cut for testing they were ten percent in moisture. When I carried those beans to the co-op, they were back up to thirteen percent, the best moisture point for them to be when you sell them! So, actually trying to destroy me, he actually helped me by doing that. Only thing was, I was disappointed that a man out there with three or four hundred acres of beans in the fields, and he would take me out of my truck, rather than write me another ticket and let me go, he would rather take me to jail and leave my truck standing out in the rain. I never did think much of the highway patrol system after that because they allowed people to do things like that.

So, I had to go then back to sheriff department and carry my canceled check to his wife, Madge Noble. She took the check and then she took action on the ticket and finally they got my license straightened out.

After that I started to hauling beans to Yazoo City. That was a little nearer than Vicksburg. I think I got one more ticket. Well I didn't get it. It was the driver (I think he was driving too fast and got it) but I had to pay it because it was my truck. After that I didn't get another ticket. In fact, I can't think of a farmer that has ever gotten a ticket unless they had a big truck overloaded and was going to Vicksburg with it. Riding the local trucks like we have here, those officers wouldn't stop us for nothing like that because they knew farmers were having a hard time with the weather and prices and it was no need for them to be imposed on us, too.

During this time, most of the black farmers, or any man that farmed as much as a hundred acres of land, would borrow money from the Farmers Home Administration or FHA (that's what it is mainly referred to). You could have those delays. They were requiring us to have insurance and of course your local ASC board members set that up. They had divided the land up in such a way that most of the black farmers yield was so low until it didn't pay you to have insurance. They insisted that if we were gone to borrow money we would have to have insurance. Most of the white farmers had a yield on their land twenty-two bushels per acres and up. The black farmer's yield was fifteen bushels. On any bad crop year you were gone make fifteen bushels. Having insurance was just another way of punishing black farmers. They had it set up that way. It was getting harder and harder to make a living on a farm. The FHA had gotten to the place that they would supervise your money. You had to go down and tell them what you wanted to spend it for. And then they would give you an appointment when to come. And if he was not there, you would not get the money. You would have to wait until he came. They just caused us black farmers to just get further and further in debt. If you were a bean farmer like I was and you needed to kill the weeds today and you had to wait two or three days later do it, the weeds would be that much bigger and it would cost much more to kill them. That's the kind of thing we had to put up with. A lot of black farmers had to go out of business. I was still hanging on and my wife wanted me to get out. But I couldn't get out. I wanted to make a big hit.

Fortunately for me, there was a gentleman from Vicksburg, his name was Atwood. He ran the Chevrolet place; he was a successful dealer. It was a place up here that we called the Cager Sutherland Place. A black preacher owned about a thousand acres up there and he died. His property was being sold. Mr. Atwood from Vicksburg bought it. Atwood had a son to move up there, but I don't think his son was much of a farmer. I think he stayed in it a while and he decided he had better get out of farming.

I thought I would be able to rent that thousand acres of land and plant it. I wound up then with about fourteen hundred acres and I still wasn't able to pay my bill. I made enough beans, if I could have gotten a decent price or if I could have gotten seven dollars a bushel at that time I would paid off all my debts and credit but it didn't happen like that.

That year the beans were down. I think I gathered over twenty-four thousand bushels and I was still in debt. My wife would continue to complain about it, rightly so.

But I remember when I was a young lad about ten years old; I was pretty large for my age. My brother and I were in the woods. We were hauling wood; we cut poles and put them on the wagon and bringing them home. I picked up a pole, I put my fingers together and locked my hands under the pole and lifted it up. And I couldn't put it down. And that's just how farming was! You get out there and then you couldn't get out of farming. I stayed out there and I scuffered around and put up with FHA. We had to go to a bank to apply for a loan. Of course, a bank wasn't going to let you have any money unless the FHA signed to give them the first lien. Therefore, the poor farmer was just given the run around. It wasn't too many black farmers around that were able to farm. Farming got harder and harder for us to stay in business. In fact, it got so bad until the government decided they would give a write-down to some of the farmers. That's when they gave me a write-down. But when they gave it to me I still wasn't much better off. But somehow or another, I never did have to file bankruptcy. I was just able to sit there and sure I would work the debt off somehow. I never did make anything on the farm. All that I did was just pure determination.

Meantime, I was in with the FHA. I still had a bill on my land and house with the Federal Land Bank. Things got so bad, they practically closed the bank down from here in Ridgeland. They had built a really nice bank. I think they had moved all of their operations from New Orleans up here. The bank was still going down. It did eventually close and they moved somewhere else. But in the meantime, while they were trying to overcome some of their ways of spending they gave us a privilege of getting another bank to buy our loan. I was fortunate enough to get at that time Citizens Bank, now it is called Bank

Plus, to buy my contract. And I was able to work it out with them. Then I still owed FHA some money but that note was not too high. The way they had it written up, if I ever get able to pay the bill off before ten years, then they would come back on me for the other. They had me tied up anyway I would go. I figured I just couldn't get away from the FHA to save my life.

My Life after the Change in Mississippi

In the meantime, another change in my life came. I can recall political ambitions getting in my way. I had run about three times. I ran against A.B. Mansell one time and I was unsuccessful. Everybody was talking about Madison County and how they count the votes up here. So what they did when I was running against A.B. Mansell, they had what you call cars-vote. They would bring the people up there in cars. Of course, they were all white that was going out there letting them vote in the cars and it was no way for you to win an election like that. That's what was happening at that time. I lost to Amos Dowdle in his second term. Then he died in the middle of that term and his wife, Dot Dowdle, she ran and won. It was a real close race. It was so close that it should have been a another election between the two of us. Alice Scott was the election commission chairperson, W.E. Garrett, and Roy Davis were on the election commission. They could have made a ruling but they didn't. It was a five-member board and the majority of three could have voted to give me the election. But they chose to call the attorney general, a white man, to make the final decision. He made a decision for the white people.

I lost that election and I was really hurt over that. I

remember returning some signs from McGraw down in Ridgeland. When I carried them back, Mr. McGraw, the owner of the rental store, had been keeping up with the results and he said, "Well, the next time they have an election, you run and you will get it next time." I was hurt about the way things had turned out. What's funny is the worst hurt a man can have is to lose an election! That's what I was up against.

I wasn't going to run anymore but I had a friend explain to me. Ike Brown's family. Ike was the head stepper in this family when it came to politics. He came to me and told me, "We are getting ready to have an election, I want you to run. Your name, McCullough, has been involved in civil rights. McCullough is a good name to run. You will have a better chance of winning because we are going to rezone the districts." He persuaded me to run. Finally, they bickered around for a while and they did. The supervisors stayed around there and they tried to fix it where the incumbent would be able to win. But so happened, where I was living, they had to make such changes that the incumbent supervisor, who at that time was Buddy Mansel, white people had gotten against him because he didn't fix the roads and the roads were in bad conditions. Most of the white people had moved out, but they had land up there and they wanted to come back and forth up there and see about it. They couldn't get up there. So, they wanted to get rid of him.

At that time, they believed that black people were not fit to be in office in a position like that. They felt that way. For some reason or another, after that redistricting, an election came about in January. When we finished that election I was able to win that election by sixty-two votes. That's when my problems really started after the election. The incumbent had allowed for all of the equipment to be destroyed. Some of the supervisors do that when they lose. We didn't have one piece of equipment running. The truck's motor and transmission was gone. The pick-up truck that he had when he was in office (he had two or three) was really good while he was in office. When it was my turn to take over nothing would run.

The motor grader would not run. Not one thing would run. I didn't have anything to work with. When I got in office there was a lady working there. Her name was Sarah Cage. She had an old piece of paper with a sign on it. I thought it was something to make a good sign to go on my pick-up truck since I was supervisor. I had on there, "Supervisor District Five, we the willing lead by the unknown, doing the impossible for the ungrateful, we have done so much for so long with so little that we are now qualified to do anything with nothing." A lot of people thought it was a funny thing but that was the way things were when I took office. I kept that sign on my truck until I retired and I finally put those signs up in my garage. They are in there now.

During this time, the sheriff, Billy Noble had just made up his mind that he was just going to get me out of office. My road foreman was Ray Parker and some of the white people had gotten him to promise to open up an old county road. He was up there working on the road. I don't know why he was just so determined to fix that road. The word came back to me that the chancery clerk, who at that time was Billy Cooper, told Ray if he would do something to help them get me out of office then they would help him to get the office. So, now I don't know if that's what he was working on or not. Anyway, while he was up there, he had a lot of equipment to fix the road with. The sheriff got a court order and seized all the equipment on that road and we had to leave it up there.

Then, the time came about when he indicted me. That threw me for a loop because I was already trying to farm and then I had to take the money that I was trying to farm with to try to defend myself.

When I first got into it I talked with Bob Montgomery about being my attorney but at that time he was the county attorney. He said he couldn't defend me and so it worked out for me. One of the things they were indicting me on was they said I was letting Joe Ross haul gravel without a bid on the job. Joe had come to me and he had explained everything to me. He was supposed to have gotten everything he needed from the Chancery Clerk. I was willing to let him haul because during that time blacks could do hardly anything for the county, especially when it came to contracts. I wanted to be able to help them get their contracts. That's what brought it on. After that, they indicted me. Then the word got out in the community that I was guilty. The word was going around that "He must be guilty otherwise they wouldn't say it."

It so happened that a white lady, Ann Hall, had been coming to the meetings complaining about her roads. I did everything to try to help her to get her roads fixed up. So when this came about, the indictments, I went to her and asked her, I said, "Mrs. Hall, I need a favor from you." She said, "Well, what is it?" I told her I wanted her to speak to a group of ministers and they were having a meeting at Mt. Zion Baptist Church in Canton. They would have that meeting of ministers every Monday. I had spoken to the moderator at that time, Rev. Perry. I had asked him about allowing a speaker to come and of course, he granted it. I came down there and told Mrs. Hall what time to be there. I was kind of worried because I never had asked a white lady for anything like that. Well, I hadn't asked them to do anything. Well, she con-

113

sented and she came up there and she did. And I tell you the truth, she did an excellent job. She told them that I was being prosecuted for nothing and she got them to believe it.

The ministers went back to their churches and put the word out about how they were just setting me up trying to get me out of office. That was the thing that really saved me. The word was spread through the community and of course, the thing that hurt me was I had to hire a lawyer, at that time Scales and Scales. It was Earnest Greer that was doing some of the hauling. Somehow, they got a hold of him. The sheriff got him and put him in jail and put him under a fifty thousand dollar bond. They told him if he testified against me, they would drop the charges. Well, he wouldn't do it so they kept him in jail.

That meant he had to get a lawyer. He had his lawyer in Jackson, Scales and Scales. When Scales came up here and got him out of jail, Greer informed me about it and told me to use Scales. And I thought then, "Well he knows what has happened so I'm going to try to hire him." I hired him to take on the case. Having been treated so bad by white people in my lifetime until I was afraid to trust him as a lawyer. So, I decided to try working with him. I didn't trust the black lawyer to go in there and I didn't trust the white lawyer. So, I called myself, getting a black lawyer, Ed Blackman, to watch the white lawyer. It worked out pretty good.

We stayed in court and finally the time came to pick the jurors. We picked a good jury. We had a choice of picking a white lady or young white man for our last juror. I didn't have any confidence in the white man as a juror. I was telling some of my fellows that were working with me that I would put my trust in the lady's hand quicker than I would in a white man's. Well, they thought he was a

114

young white man and that he would be fair. It turned out just like I thought it would. The jurors all voted, eleven to one, and that one that held out was that white man. In the end, it was eleven to one for an acquittal.

To tell you the truth, when I came out of the courthouse that day, I had a lot of people there. I really didn't know I had that many friends, a lot of white people. Mrs. Hall, she was supporting me. I really had good support. I want to thank all those people today for being there for me during my trying time. When I came out after the jurors reached a decision, I came down the stairs, I can recall how I felt. It was a feeling of being crucified. I said as I came down the stairs, "As I descend from the cross of crucifixion, my head is bloody but unbowed." What I was feeling then was all that they had done to me was bloody my head a little and I was still able to walk away from the court proud. That was the thing.

It continued like that. The sheriff even put a deputy, Tim Hudson, up in my district. And his job was to follow my road crew every day and see what did we do. They attacked me again. They still had another charge on me. But the judge threw it out. Judge Goza tried me. But what I found out later was what usually happened; the judge that was in the county didn't try supervisors. However, by me being black and unknowing he tried me. He read the rules to the jurors urging them to find me guilty. But so happened they didn't. I was able to get out of that.

This is what Judge Nichols ruled, "In the circuit court of Madison County, Mississippi, the State of Mississippi versus Jessie J.L. McCullough on this day the above styling number caused come on for a hearing on the state's request for consent to knowingly prosecutor and the courts have examined saying and being of the opinion that such request is reasonable in that same should be

115

granted it is therefore ordered that the above style and number cause shall be and the same is hereby dismissed and further that the state's request shall consent to knowingly prosecutor when considered with this order shall be deemed sufficient interest of the knowingly prosecutor by the state it is so ordered this the 26th day of August 1985." Albert Nichols/Circuit Judge. Prepared and submitted by Aubrey Craft/District Attorney.

The next thing they did was to put the state auditor on me. This lady was named Mary Dixon that came up here. She went back and she finally came up with a fine on me for $1,142.98. Now, I had to pay that. After the audit was over, in 1987 I went back to the state auditor and asked them to give me my money back. At some point in the boardroom we had had a discussion that this particular road was a county road and it had been worked on. The state auditors informed me that they had sent the money back to the county supervisors and I needed to ask the board to give me my money back. After all of the litigation was over, Pat Luckett who was on the board said, "Well, I think we ought to give J.L. his money back. They did used to work that road and they never did take it off the county map." Therefore, they gave me the money back that they had charged me, which was $1,142.98. They took me through all that and in the end the county had to give me my money back. By following the rules and trying to be right all the time paid off for me.

About this time, the federal government had set up a sting operation in the state. They had a lot of makeshift companies that were going around seducing supervisors to engage in illegal activities. The supervisor would obtain goods from these makeshift companies for a lower price than they were reporting on their purchase orders. The difference in the actual price of the goods and what the county was billed for the products was put in the supervisor's pocket. If they didn't have anything to sell they just pretended that they had something to sell. If you sent in the purchase order then you had broken the law.

That time of the year, all of the supervisors usually met in Biloxi. That year I was staying at the Hilton Hotel. The agent was from Mississippi State; I believe his name was P.C. McLaurin and he was directing the activities of the Supervisors Association. He had encouraged all the supervisors to patronize all the businesses that had their exhibits there. They were all in line and we were going around looking at each exhibit. Some of them were picking up some little gifts that they had, little whatnots.

I ran up on a fellow whose organization was called the Davis Chemical Company. He was supposed to be a small operator. I found out later he was an agent for the FBI. At the time at the association in Biloxi, nobody knew that. When I talked with him he told me about what a hard time small companies have and how hard it was to compete with these large companies. Well, I knew that. In fact I bought some chemicals from him that we used to spray the roadside with. He was trying to get me to buy more and I told him, "No, this is all they allow us to buy without a purchase order." He kept talking and talking. I told him I couldn't do that. I couldn't buy anymore anyway because we couldn't buy stuff to store up because our district was the poorest district in the county. At that time we were in what we called the beat system.

Like I said, P.C. McLaurin advised us to patronize as many as we could. When they have these associations, each one usually has hospitality rooms. The Democratic party had one and the Republican party had one and any number of companies had hospitality rooms. I went to all of them; I even went to the Republican's. When I came

117

out, I said, "Well, let me go by Davis." I was passing by and I said, "Let me go in here and see what Davis is talking about." When I got there we got to talking. During that time all the football teams in the country were getting ready for the fall football season. We hit off on that topic and we had a good discussion on who we thought would be the best team.

Then he began to tell me about how we could make some money. I told him I was not concerned about making any money because I wasn't even thinking about nothing like that. He said, "You know, if you would buy more of this chemical and then we could fix it where you could make some money."

I told him, "Well, no, I can't do that. I've been telling you all the time that I can't invest in anything that we don't need to use right away. I can't afford to tie up the money in something that I don't need. I need the money to be there if there is something we just absolutely have to do."

We kept on talking and we talked a long time. Everything he talked about was making money . . . making money. Well, I didn't realize that he had his microphone and was recording what was said. But I kept telling him, "No, we can't afford it."

Everything he said was about making money. When I got ready to leave, he had a bunch of stuff wrapped up in a basket setting there. He said, "Get one of those presents and take it to your wife."

I just picked it up and held it in my hand. He said, "Aren't you gone look at it?"

I said, "Well, whatever it is she'll be happy." I didn't look at it; I stuck it in my pocket and walked on out. I got back to my room or I think I had made it home before I opened it. I have a habit of not opening things. And when

118

I opened it I saw that it was forty dollars. I said, "Well, there is nothing I can do about it now. I don't know what I can do with the forty dollars." I spent it somewhere.

He came up here to my house and all his talk was "We can make some money." He had the same line about "what I would want you to buy." I told him, "No, we just can't afford it. " And we talked and I guess he was here about an hour. I didn't ever commit to him and so he finally left. He came back again. And we talked again. The last time I can remember him coming, he came and it was kind of misting rain and so I told him that I didn't want to stand out in the rain so I told him to come on in the kitchen.

We sat down in the kitchen and we talked. He laid a hundred-dollar bill on the table and said, "You can take this hundred dollars and we could start from there. Maybe we could work out something where you and I both could make some money."

I told him, "No, I can't do anything. You take your money. I told you I'll buy from you when I need something. I'll do that. I realize you are a good salesman to keep pushing like that but this is just something we don't need and I can't do it. But when I need something, I'll be sure to call on you."

He left and he never did get me to commit. About two years later, I was out here getting ready to go to the fields. I had a couple of fellows helping me trying to get finished planting. With two others helping me I figured I would get through really soon. Most of the time, I drove one tractor and another fellow drove another. This time we were going to use three. So we were all standing around out there getting ready.

This fellow pulled up here in his car. He came over

there where I was and asked for me. He asked, "Is this J.L. McCullough?"

I said, "Yes."

"I want to talk with you," he said.

I said, "Start talking." I thought he was one of those salesmen.

He said, "I don't think you want these fellows to hear it."

"Well, let us walk out here to this tree," I said. It was a persimmon tree out there by my gas tank. We started talking and he showed me his badge that he was a law enforcer. He started playing a tape. The tape was supposedly of what I had said about how the money would come up if I had said I would take the money. And I was going to co-operate. The way he had it played back, he had cut out what I said and had put in, in such a way that would sound like I had agreed to it.

So, I told him, "That's not what I said."

He said, "You can't remember what you said two years ago."

And I said, "The hell I can't! If you ask me the same question, I'll give you the same damn answer!" When I told him that and what I actually had said, he stayed there a little while and then he finally left. I never did see him anymore. I know that somebody from the auditor's office went down to the county office and took the records but nothing was ever said to me.

It came out in all of the newspapers that this man was an agent for the government and anyone who had bought the stuff from him would be in trouble. Well, I had bought some from him but I had done it legally. I bought as much as I could without a purchase order and that's all that I had. After that I never did hear anything from it anymore.

It rocked on and another gentleman from Natchez who was a salesman, his name was Key. He was the one warned me about all the stuff that was going on. He didn't tell me about the sting but he told me that it was people coming around and giving you kickbacks. He even told me though he was trying to sell me something. I told him, "Well, if you got a discount, give it to the county. We don't have that much money."

Nine

Anyway, It was Mr. Key who had enlightened me on all the things that was going on. I guess I need to say thanks to him today. No doubt, if it hadn't been for him, they would have probably gotten a chance to get me out of office when the sheriff was trying so hard before. By him warning me like he did, that saved me, I know.

Now, during this time, one of our supervisors died, Mr. Pat Luckett. He had started and gotten about halfway through the term when I was in office. Of course, they brought it to the board president, Julius Harris. We referred to him all the time as Brother Harris. We met there and the supervisors had an opportunity at that time to name a person to replace Pat until the election was held. But we couldn't agree. The president, Brother Harris wanted to go on tradition. Tradition said they should appoint the supervisor's wife. But I had grown up under that magic word of *tradition* and I'd witnessed some black men being electrocuted because of tradition. To me, tradition was meant to prosecute black people. I just couldn't vote for tradition. So, we met and met and met until finally the papers started writing so bad about me. I decided to answer some of the letters and the editors in the paper. This is the letter that I wrote to them in February 14, 1989:

After the letters about Mrs. Luckett ran in the newspaper, I am compelled to respond. First, it is necessary for me to inform the public of the negotiation that has taken place since Mr. Luckett's death. I was prepared to name a successor for Mr. Luckett on the first day we met. But I was and still am against voting on tradition. I feel that tradition discriminates; therefore, I will not vote against my belief. I remain flexible. I refuse to name a black person because the whites probably call me a racist. I refuse to name a white person because the blacks will probably say that I caved in. I have met with President Harris a number of times to try for a compromise. But he only offers the same name, Mrs. Luckett. I have met Mrs. Luckett and I think she is a very sweet lady. I'm not voting against her, I am voting against tradition. Supervisor Banks offered a proposal that could possibly have solved the problem. He suggested that we allow persons who are interested in the position to submit their resumes and the choice could be made from this group. President Harris and supervisor Richardson considered the suggestion. I will make one and only one offer and that is that four or five names be submitted that they feel comfortable with and allow us the chance to review with them the issue at hand. Either this, or I will wait for the November election. The Unit System was voted in last November. We have not done one thing toward making plans for change over. First of all, there seems to be a feeling that we cannot work with the press present. We have more secrets than the Pentagon. As of this day, I will not condone any more secrets unless it is legal matters or strictly personnel. If I am out-voted I will personally report it to the news media. J.L. McCullough.

Now with the unit system being closer and closer to the time for us to put it into effect, we discussed it time and time again.

The president said he wasn't prepared to vote on it

until we had five members on the board. I didn't feel like that was the thing to do. I felt like four could agree. Only thing would be, we would have more compromise than we would if we had five. I was more concerned about that. So we never did get the unit system organized; in fact, it's not organized today. One of the reasons that it's not organized, hadn't any of the other members of the board had any experience in dealing with a lot of people and really to know what the unit system looked like. But I'd had an opportunity to work with different construction companies and manufactories. I had a good idea of what needed to be done to organize the unit system to make it effective. They refused to allow me opportunity to present my plan even though I had drawn up a plan on paper where you could see each step that had to be taken. Of course, they wouldn't take it up. That day we left without doing anything. So, the next meeting came up and the chancery clerk, Billy Cooper, had him a plan. Now, before he didn't have one. See, he was able to copy off mine. But we never did do anything and the unit system of Madison County today does not work.

Now, during this time, the road department was not servicing the community and it's not being serviced now. For some reason some of the supervisors think you ought to spend all of the money down on the south end of Madison County. And that's wrong. If that was the way government worked, Mississippi would hardly get any federal money to be spent here because they put less up there in the treasury than any other state. But that is not the way it should be done. I didn't feel like that, yet I was never able to convert my co-workers that was the better thing to do.

For another reason the unit system didn't work, to begin with, we didn't have experience to develop it. Only one supervisor had that knowledge and that was *me*. We would always make the choice of the man to be road manager, well at that time it was based on friendship. The first road manager was Tim Irving who was Robert Dowdle's buddy. I voted for him because he was young and thought we could train him but that didn't work. Then we chose Tommy Faulkner to be a road manager. That didn't work because he didn't have the experience nor training to do this. Then we hired a man from Jackson named Russell Doras. Doras had the knowledge to do it but he was so wrapped up in himself that he never did get the road department organized right. When he did work, he did most of the work in one area, which was unacceptable to the county. I continued to complain to them about the road department not performing like it was supposed to. I guess the people with no knowledge of how it was supposed to work thought it was working fine.

During that time some of the supervisors were upset and weren't pleased with our secretary, the board's secretary, who was, at the time, Lee Westbrook. I thought she had done a good job. I always thought she was helpful with whatever we needed. I just couldn't see getting rid of her. But they had enough votes to get rid of her. Three votes was all that was needed. Richardson, Dowdle and Sharp. They wanted her out.

We replaced her with a lady who had been working for the Madison County Herald. We hired her. We were saying that there was a chance that she would give us good public relations for the county. When she came on she was working somewhere in the mall and would do county work at night, which was impossible. During the day when we would get all the calls in from different companies about what we owed them or something that had to be done from eight o'clock until five o'clock, she needed to be there. And she said she could do our work at night, but she couldn't. She couldn't answer the phone at night because no one would call at night. She worked on there for a while. Her term was short-lived. Her name was Deborah Montgomery.

The chancery clerk recommended Kathy and she was a good secretary. Our trouble continued with our road department.

This time my fourth election came up and we had a controversy over it. That was while Deborah was still secretary. Then came in Millard Beamon. He contested the election and said he should be in the runoff with me. It was held up in court and we followed around for a year trying to get that settled. In the meantime, Timmy Pickett began to fight because he knew he had won over Millard and if they were going to have an additional election he knew he should be in the runoff. There we were trying to get *that* settled. This went on for a year. We had two new supervisors to take their seat without controversy, Louise Spivey and Walter Waldrup.

During that time I was still serving until the position was filled. We started to work together and I thought we would be able to guide the board in the right direction. When Louise came on they wanted to change the attorney for the county. They wanted Jim Herring. And of course, Bob Montgomery had stood by me during all of my crisis and I couldn't see myself not supporting a man who had supported me when I desperately needed help. I told them right off. When they got elected, they came to my house to discuss it and I told them, "Every thing is on the table except one thing. That is Bob. I'm not going to vote to get rid of Bob. He has done so much to help me when I was having so many problems with the sheriff and everything. I just can't do that." Well, that didn't please Louise.

However, we did agree to do something constructive. We decided to rotate the position of president on the board. That meant that we would share; one person would serve one year. It would go around to all. It was something that was legal and was being done all over the state. Walter Waldrup wanted to serve first and we agreed and I was supposed to serve the second year. Walter had quite a controversial year. When it came time for me to serve, I took over and I came up with a good proposal. I felt we should fix up all the roads and in order to fix some roads we would have to fix some streets. In order to get my program through I needed to go to the legislature and get special local and private bill to carry out my plan. I had gotten to the legislature and met with Charlie Williams who was chairman of the Ways and Means Committee. He advised me that he would do that. Things were about to shape up.

During that time Louise began to fight my plan. Well, at first she was going along with it. Then something happened and she decided not to go along with it. So, she didn't. She went down and talked with the state representative, Rita Martinson, and persuaded her not to sponsor it for me. One day while we were down in the capital building, we had agreed on everything because Charlie Williams, who over the Ways and Means Committee said, "As long as you all agree, I don't have a problem with that."

That's where the problem came in when she decided that she could no longer support the idea. She had gotten a letter and convinced Rita Martinson, Edward Blackmon and Barbara Blackmon to sign it which said that they would not sponsor the bill. That tore up the plan. What really made it look good for me was how I was going about it. Louise said if I would get that bill through they couldn't defeat me. So, she had decided to work against me.

The Madison County Journal made this statement about it: "McCullough has a good set of priorities, although the meeting of the Madison County Board of Supervisors has not been so rowdy as those of the Jackson City Counsel. They have had their tense moments so it is some relief that incumbent president, J.L. McCullough, has a set of priorities in mind for the board to accomplish while he is in power. They include a comprehensive plan to repair all streets and roads in Madison County. This is necessary to bring Madison County up to the level of the highly populated place in the county. The green pasture and railroad that used to be so scenic and tranquil are now packed with commuters rushing to Jackson. Better and wider school roads are needed. A standard salary for employees and pay scale compatible with the private sector. Good workers should be rewarded and retained and not have to rely on politics for salary. Good county workers should be courteous and helpful to constituents and prompt with their work. Good communication between citizens and members of government should bring about better service. The goals set by McCullough are sound and if he is successful in implementing them, he will have accomplished much."

After Louise started disagreeing with the plan, she was determined that she was going to defeat me and elect Pickett. She was going around campaigning for him and I think she had a little organization to help raise money for him. She had gone up in the communities out in my district and calling and doing everything she could to try to get me defeated. I was going around amongst my people talking with them like I have always done. This was the beginning of my fourth term. I was out there after the primaries were over. I was going back reminding people to come out to the polls again. While I was out there I ran into a lot of white people and they told me Louise had told them, "Don't vote for J.L. this time; vote for Pickett. J.L. has a mind of his own. If you elect Pickett, he will do what I say." Therefore, she was out working trying to get Pickett elected. However, it ran almost to the last of August before we got it settled and we didn't get to accomplish anything I had planned.

In the election, Millard Beamon was eliminated *again*. So it was left up to Pickett and me again. In the end, I tried to get the election commissioner to put it off until the regular election in November. They weren't going to do that. They were determined to get rid of me, some of them. They met that Friday and decided to have the election on that following Tuesday. But what they didn't know, I had all of my people informed and Pickett was working on a job every day and he didn't have his people informed about when the election was going to take place. When the election came up, that Tuesday my people came out and his didn't. I won the election by a landslide. That ended the election. But it brought disarray on the board. Louise was not happy with the way things went and the board just started falling apart. We never did get together where we could do any real service for the county. In the shuffle, Louise didn't get the following in her district that she needed. She had created some powerful enemies in her district and they were determined to get rid of her. And they did. So that ended her career. At the end, I was going to retire anyway, and I did. In the meantime, all these things were going on.

There were days I would ride out over the county, first one district and another to see what needed to be done. So, this day I was riding down in Supervisor Richardson's district. I had seen it once before and complained about it. I got there this time and I pulled in there behind his motor grader so that he couldn't move. I walked up there and chastised him and asked him to get off the motor grader and let the workers have their own machine to go to work. Of course, when I did that, he was up on the machine above my head and he kicked down on my shoulder and I was upset about that.

So, I had to go to court with him. And I did. I had some friends that had encouraged me to go to court. So, I was planning on when we were going to have it out because I was brought up never to take a lick from a white man. If you do get into a fight with a white man make sure that you fight until you die or until you whip him. If you couldn't whip him, you would have to report to God . . . why not? I took him to court and the court found David guilty. I decided to live with the court's decision like a good citizen should do. That was the court's decision. I didn't have to go back because I had *really* planned to jump on David in the boardroom. But since the court ruled like it did, you know, most time before that when a black man would come in court with a white man they wouldn't do anything. But this court had made the right decision. After the court made its ruling like they should have then I accepted the verdicts.

David Richardson was elected at the same time on the board that Karl Banks and I were elected. The white people had kind of painted David to be what they called a "nigger lover." I didn't want to see that stigma attached to David because I knew if that was attached to him that meant a kiss of death for a politician in Mississippi. So, I did everything I could to avoid showing any kind of friendship with David out in the public. In the boardroom I would shake hands with the other supervisors, yet, I would never shake hands with David. I never did mention it to him because I was doing everything to protect him. I just hate to see something like that kill a man's career. I did everything I could to protect David. In the end, I never would have thought David would have acted like he did. But that's the way things ended.

The accomplishments I am most proud of while I was on the board was when I was elected the hospital had stopped delivering babies in Canton. I was instrumental in getting the hospital to deliver babies again. The farmers couldn't take their produce to market because the bridges were not good. I was able to build twenty. I was able to get countywide garbage pick-up. I helped to establish the water system up in the northeast part of the county. Sheriff Noble died and I was able to help elect a new sheriff, Jessie Hopkins. In the end he wasn't able to manage his department like the county needed. Of course, I regretted that. But afterward I was able to help elect a man who had the welfare of the county at heart and the ability to manage the department, Sheriff Toby Trowbridge, and for that, I am grateful. I was able to help get in a chancery clerk who has done a wonderful job for Madison County, Steve Duncan. I am proud of that because he has done so much to upgrade the process for keeping records for the county. I will always be grateful for the service he rendered to Madison County.

During all of the places that I worked, I can't think of a more appreciative staff than I had at the Madison County Chancery Clerk building. All the ladies there were always trying to be helpful. They were so nice in every way. They just seemed to be a family. I guess that's what it was. Shirley Cole was the oldest one there and I considered her my oldest daughter. Of course, the rest were just part of my big family. I had a special relationship with Kathy Gregory, I considered her my naughty brat. To look back at this, one of the happiest memories of my life was a staff that appreciated what I tried to do. So much that, even now when I go by there I still feel a closeness; I always make a point to try to blame Kathy for something that has happened and most of the time blame her for things that have not happened. It is just such a good relationship that I just enjoyed meeting them and knowing them and it always seems that they enjoyed meeting me. They were a wonderful staff. I hated to say good-bye to a staff like that. Yet, I still have wonderful memories of them.

And now a special thanks to those who helped me so much in my political career: Ike Brown for persuading me to run the four times that I ran; Bob Montgomery for my special counsel during my trying times; CC or Brother Clarence (we called him Bear) and his wife, Sarah, because he always worked the Canton Precinct very successfully; James Goodloe and his wife, Jimmie Mae, they always found a way to make a contribution to my campaign; and Albert Catching who was always loyal to me and worked hard any way he could to make my political career a success; Percy Honeysucker was always there in my campaign and worked hard for me to succeed; and Joseph Harris who traveled all over the district during my campaign urging people to elect me; and to the Sims family, Edward and his wife, Maggie Mae, for encouraging their family and using all of their influence in the community to help get me re-elected; Steve Duncan and his wife, LeAnne, they played a great part in helping me get elected, too, (Steve not only helped me get re-elected, he played a major role in helping to get some projects done in district 5), and I just want to take this time to say a special thanks to all those people who made such a contribution to make my political career a success.

Now a special tribute to my family: my wife, Kattie, for standing by me through all of my crises, my father who taught me to work, and my mother who taught me to be honest. The lessons that she taught me from the incidents that happened in my life were part of what gave me the good character that I have. Back in the days when marbles was king, I had some cousins that would steal my marbles and anybody else's and they would get away with it. So, late one night my mother, (usually the families in the community borrowed from one another, flour, sugar, etc.) sent me over there for one of those items. It was late that night when I came through and Edward had gone to bed and left his clothes hanging on a chair and of course, his marbles were hanging on his over-alls on a chair in a tobacco sack. I snatched and broke the string off it and put it in my pocket. I went on home and when I got there I put them in a dresser drawer. Mother heard me, she didn't know what I was doing but she heard me. Well, the next morning Edward came over there and told my mother that I had stolen his marbles and she called me in and told me to go get those marbles. I told her I didn't have them but she said, "Go in there and look in that dresser drawer in that room where you were last night and get those marbles and bring them *here*." So, I went and got them and she gave me a good whipping and she made me take them back to him and told me to tell them that I stole them. Well, that was too hard a pill for me to swallow. Because she wasn't there, I told him that my brother, Willot, stole them. You see, Willot didn't steal them; I stole them. That's one of the greatest lessons that a mother could teach a child.

My sister, Eeula, was so special. She encouraged me

so much to continue my education even though I had fallen behind. And I was so far behind that I didn't want to go back to school. Of course, I want to thank my Uncle Charlie for his message of inspiration to me. Eeula would always do whatever she thought would encourage me to continue my education. She used what she had to take care of me; she fed me; she furnished me a room downtown with her and just encouraged me to the highest to continue. I'm not sure whether she did that because she dropped out of school or if she just wanted someone in the family to finish high school. So, she was able to get me to stay in school. I have to say "thank you" to her today because she is the reason that I have an education today and am making the contributions to society that I've been able to make. **Thank you, Sister, thank you!** I will remind you that I was *twenty-three* when I finished high school.